FROM YONDER TO HERE

THE LIFE AND WORK OF
DR. OZELL SUTTON

To Jemima

BY VIC CARTER

From Yonder to Here

The Life and Work of Dr. Ozell Sutton

© 2008 by Lee-Com Media Services, LLC

From Yonder to Here
The Life and Work of
Dr. Ozell Sutton
By Vic Carter

DEDICATION

My life's journey has two major sponsors. Of course there were many more who contributed to my being me, but I have to give the majority of the credit to two women who have been the mainstay of my life, my inspiration, my love. The first, of course, gave to me this wonderful thing we call life. Lula Belle brought me into this world and she never let me forget she also could take me out of it. There is no love greater than that of a mother. Most assuredly if you take into account the fact that Lula had to share that love with seven other children. For most of my life she reared us by herself since my father passed away when I was very young. In the 1930's that required a special mix of love, affection, guidance, wisdom, and nerves of steel. Lula Belle kept each of us aware of who we are, where we are, and our responsibility to each other, and to those with whom we share the world. Many a lesson was learned from this woman by me and my siblings. The greatest of which had to be that every man is equal, none greater than the other, none lesser. Her words ring in my ears and beckon me to continue to fight for those in need and suffering and mistreated. She was one, who suffered and was mistreated, but still she pressed on and I saw that. She instilled in me the notion that I must be of service until I can give no more. Her lessons and her words were strength to me in those weary days of the Civil Rights Movement. Never did I waiver, nor concern myself with what was the right thing to do. I knew my mission and my purpose for being. Thank you Lula Belle for planting in me the seed that grew - as in the words of the spiritual – "like a mighty tree planted by the river – I shall not be moved."

Where Lula Belle gave me vigor, an equally magnificent woman taught me to be tender and kind and gentle. Joanna Velda Rose Freeman is like her namesake flower that grows among the thorns. Even amid tumultuous times, Joanna would always bring me back to the center. I knew it the first time I saw her, a young pretty thing who was equally shy and strong at the same time. She was the one. I was rough around the edges, straightforward, quick witted and prepared to say whatever came to my mind. Joanna has always been thoughtful and concerned not only for me but also for the three beautiful women we reared. Joanna never joined me on the road during the civil rights movement. If she had been with me, there is no way I could have practiced non-violence. Had one cross word been said to her, the marine would have rushed up from the depths of my soul and would have lashed out with a fury untold. She understood this and also knew that I would rarely tell her the whole story of what I endured while on the road. I knew she would worry, so to her, I would say, "I am just fine, Joanna. How are you and my little sweet girls?" Angela, Tena, and Dietre are even today – my sweet little girls. Joanna was my eyes and ears when I was away from the home. She was the disciplinarian and she was the one who wiped away the tears if knee was scrapped or friend had somehow hurt someone's feelings. I would always check in by phone and promise to come right home as soon as I could get there. These women were never far from my mind, even when I was being beaten in the streets by white police officers or being called a variety of names by the Klan or some equally racist mob.

Joanna, "thank you my love," for giving me the freedom to pursue my dream. Thank you for being my support and for keeping my mind focused on the little things as well as these big ones.

If I were standing before a crowd of people telling this story, Joanna would seek my attention, catch my eye and pretend to blow me a kiss. The audience would coo, thinking this was a show of affection. Only I would know its true meaning. It is something she developed a long time ago. It was actually a signal – admonishing me to "K.I.S.S." – "Keep it short stupid"!

And with that, I shall move on.

FROM THE COAUTHOR
VIC CARTER

As a journalist, and particularly when you are early in your career, you always wonder about the one story that will propel your career; the one that people will see and notice that you had the edge; that you were in the right place at the right time; and that you handled your "good fortune" with skill, accuracy, and fairness. You don't wish it to happen, that is useless. Instead, you bide your time and cover the news of the day knowing that some of these stories will one day be seen by someone who sees something in you. Along the way you meet people who influence your work. Sometimes those are people in your field – the reporter who is the better writer and thus a better storyteller; the journalist who always seems to know the right thing to say and the right way to say it. Then there are the people you cover, who give you the interview. They range from those at the highest levels of government to the man or woman on the street who is simply hoping to make it through the day with what they have. Everyone in between, in some way or another shapes the kind of reporter you are and gives you an insight to life that you otherwise might miss because of the demands of your day and the pressure to tell yet another story on deadline.

I have been blessed to have covered a wide range of stories in thousands of cities and towns, in more than a dozen countries and on four continents. I have been in the company of Presidents of the United States and newly elected members of small town school boards. I have interviewed Academy Award winners and the lead actors in the holiday program at elementary schools. Each experience is different and I learned something from everybody. All of those experiences can hardly compare to my meeting the man whose memoirs I recorded and transcribed for this book.

On November 3, 1979, I was 22 years old and working as a reporter for WRAL-TV in Raleigh, North Carolina. I happened to stop by the station that Saturday morning and was startled by the clanging of the bells on the Associated Press and United Press International wire machines. I ran up and saw the headlines. "Shooting in Greensboro". "KKK and Communists Workers Party Shootout – four people dead".

I notified the on-call manager and summoned our helicopter. In a matter of moments I was off for Greensboro. After arriving and seeing some of the chaos in the aftermath, my crew and I went to High Point, North Carolina, and viewed the tapes shot by our affiliate there. Clear as day I saw the guns come out – the shots fired and the bodies falling. Over the next few days I covered this story nonstop. Soon thereafter I got a tip that the Department of Justice was sending the F.B.I. and Community Relations officials to monitor the investigation and to ensure that more violence did not occur.

There was a news briefing on the steps of the Guilford County Courthouse to announce the federal involvement. There was an African American man standing there whom I recognized. Surely I thought this would give me an edge over all the other reporters. Here was someone I knew in the federal government who knew the inside story. The question was – how do I get to him – alone and break the ice? The man was Ozell Sutton, and I knew him because he was the 26th General President of my fraternity, Alpha Phi Alpha. In the fraternity we have a saying called "leaning on the shield" – meaning – using the fraternity alliance to call in a favor – a hookup!

After the news conference I decided to ease my way up to Ozell and hoping he would see this reporter and offer him some tidbit of information. So I introduced myself and left out the fraternal connection. I told him about a little incident of which I was aware hoping to get his reaction for my story and possibly tell him something he didn't know. Ozell, being a wise and experienced federal official and my being a young and lightly experienced reporter – took the opportunity to tell me, "Young man, there is nothing you can tell me that I don't already know! But nice try!"

With that, Ozell flashed his million-watt smile and tapped me on the back. I told him of our fraternal connection and the smile got bigger. He still didn't tell me anything, but he was kind and understanding. Ozell Sutton is not one who easily strays from his convictions. I admire that in him. Over the years we came to know each other better, especially when I moved to Atlanta to work for WSB-TV. Ozell was the director of the office of Community Relations for the Department of Justice. His office was in the Citizens Trust Bank Building on Piedmont near downtown.

While in Atlanta, I joined the historic Friendship Baptist Church on Mitchell Street near the Atlanta University Center – and there sat Ozell Sutton. I knew I was in the right place.

Ozell and his wife Joanna and their entire family have been great friends and inspirations. Ozell is never without a smile, never without a story, and never without the time to stop and to talk to even the least of these. Ozell has great peripheral vision. He sees everyone, talks to anyone and somehow knows the right thing to say at the right time. Ozell loves his wife, adores his family and praises his God – strengths that helped him to endure some painful and life threatening episodes.

Over a year and a half, I traveled back and forth from Baltimore to Atlanta, sat in Ozell's basement for hours at a time and listened to him talk. I would tap away at my laptop computer jotting down his quips and comments as quickly as I could. Somehow, when Ozell talks about his life, it does not come across with the slightest element of conceit. Now do not get me wrong. Ozell loves Ozell, as well he should. He also knows that there are lessons in his stories that can benefit others. If there is anything that I have learned from Ozell, it is that our histories are important. We need to tell our own stories. We need to share our experiences. Few people will have the level of drama that Ozell has experienced, but we all have life lessons to tell. We all have stories that are worth preserving and sharing from one generation to the next.

His is a collection of vignettes that we have tried to pull together. There are admittedly some gaps in time and the order may not be chronological, but each of the stories he tells is important. I think you will agree that the contributions of Ozell Sutton and of thousands upon thousands of people like him have long gone unrecognized and in some cases unrecorded. Ozell is a contributor to the history of the nation. He is revered by those who know him as a soldier in the fight for civil rights. He is an underseen icon whose work was out of the spotlight, but nevertheless there, nevertheless important.

I am honored to have had the opportunity to help Ozell tell his story in a more complete form. Most of all, I am honored by his confidence in me and the friendship he has shown. I love Ozell Sutton as a member of my family and the family of man. Here now is his story – a journey that takes a small boy on a sharecropper's farm – "From Yonder to Here".

"44"

(Photo Courtesy of Tom Beach)

"I, Barack Hussein Obama, do solemnly swear that I will faithfully execute the office of President of the United States, and will to the best of my ability, preserve, protect and defend the Constitution of the United States of America. So help me God!"

I never thought those words would cross the lips of a man whose skin color resembled mine. It is a thought that has permeated the black community for hundreds of years. A black president?

I am blessed to have lived more than four score. In my lifetime, I have seen through my eyes, the struggle and the suffering that led to January 20, 2009. It has been my lifelong mission to usher in the era that would make this type of accomplishment a reality.

My wife and I sat in our dimly-lit in front of the glow of our television set as did millions of Americans...on election night and then again on Inauguration day. We silently wept tears of joy. Tears were shed for the accomplishments of

1

President Obama, yet there were tears of sorrow for those who endured the struggle but who did not live long enough to witness this historic moment. Their spirits were there. Their hands were there, gently placed on his shoulders giving him the strength of those who paved the way and whose aura will dwell in and around him.

During that weekend he spoke from the very steps where Dr. Martin Luther King, Jr. spoke during the great March on Washington – looking out upon the masses dwarfed by the alabaster marble image of the 16th President of the United States. He stood there – his right shoulder pointed in the direction of where a memorial to Dr. King will be erected during his term and under the direction of Alpha Phi Alpha Fraternity, Inc. and the Congress of the United States.

God has placed this man in power at a necessary time. It is a time of conflict and a time of uncertainty for America. Beneath the unfurled flags of the nation's capitol, he spoke with a clarity and a volume, and words that stretched well into the future – but yet gently touches the past in homage to his present and his future. He stood in the shadow of a massive dome that was built by the hands of slaves. He lives in a home that was constructed on the backs of indentured servants. Into the hands of the descendants of those slaves is entrusted its care.

On January 20, 2009 President Obama recalled our past and the struggles of this nation – he spoke:

> *In reaffirming the greatness of our nation we understand that greatness is never a given. It must be earned. Our journey has never been one of short-cuts or settling for less. It has not been the path for the faint-hearted, for those that prefer leisure over work, or seek only the pleasures of riches and fame. Rather, it has been the risk-takers, the doers, the makers of things -- some celebrated, but more often men and women obscure in their labor – who have carried us up the long rugged path towards prosperity and freedom.*
> – President Barack Obama

The rugged path is one with which I am truly familiar. It is one I have witnessed through these dark eyes and one which left a mark on me that shall only fade with my passing. I salute my president. I wish him well as he leads this nation out of some troubling times and into a brighter future. I say this because I know that path of this nation and the fact that his being elected is nothing short of a miracle. It is one though that was forged by the very first black people to register to vote. It was born out of the vestiges of a country bound to keep people of color "in their place". I love what I have been able to do for my country. Were it not for the work of people like me – there would be no Barack Obama – President of the United States. His victory is our victory. Millions of Americans lost their lives to insure this moment in history. Godspeed Mr. President – you are our bright hope.

America: In the face of our common dangers, in this winter of our hardship, let us remember these timeless words. With hope and virtue, let us brave once more the icy currents, and endure what storms may come. Let it be said by our children's children that when we were tested we refused to let this journey end, that we did not turn back nor did we falter; and with eyes fixed on the horizon and God's grace upon us, we carried forth that great gift of freedom and delivered it safely to future generations. Thank you. God bless you. And God bless the United States of America.

(Applause.)

Frederick Douglass High School
Atlanta, Georgia

From my seat on the stage at Frederick Douglass High School, a predominantly black high school in southwest Atlanta, I gaze into eyes that never shall see the struggle of the life I have lived. They will never experience the turmoil of a people who weathered a mighty storm that allows them to sit in the comfort of this auditorium. I wonder if they know they were loved so much that people gave their lives for a freedom still not fully realized. They were people who never knew their names, but yet they risked all they had because they knew there was a generation to come. I wonder if they are aware of their power to make change. I will rise in a moment from my seat next to Dr. William Cosby as we honor a man whose struggle helped to change this nation, the Reverend Joseph Lowery. Lowery is the founder of the Southern Christian Leadership Conference and a pastor whose voice reverberates from pulpits in churches large and small. He too will deliver a message of struggle, progress, challenge, and hope. But first, I must prick the consciousness of this young audience and cause them to think about more than their classes, computers, ipods or the lyrics to the latest tunes. As I look at them, I see exuberant energy and promise; but sometimes it is difficult for me to see that. Their sagging pants that drag the floor and loud relentless music is sometimes a distraction. I know those things are important to them, but so are the lessons of our past. The stories of our heritage allow us the freedoms of this hour.

It states on the program that I am to give an interpretation of "Lift Ev'ry Voice and Sing" written by James Weldon Johnson. It is the song of our liberation and our song of praise. We have dubbed it the Negro National Anthem. We have come through many tough times with this word, "Negro." This anthem is sung at gatherings celebrating our heritage and celebrating each other. So often, we sing the words, but we never give the lyrics their due. We rarely give thought to the three distinct messages of this hymn. First and foremost, it is a song of praise – "Lift Ev'ry voice and sing, till earth and heaven ring..." Secondly, it is a song that acknowledges our struggle – "Stony the road we trod, bitter the chastening rod..." Then there in that third verse, we are challenged to stay the course, never stray from our purposes in life and remember the incredible God who made it so – "...Thou who has by thy might, led us into the light..." Three distinct messages buried in the words that proclaim so much for us; so much about us; so much that will be the predictor of our future.

Today, I will try to make these young ears hear the words, understand and know their meaning, and embrace their purpose. When I think of the words of this anthem, their messages reach deep down in my soul. Those words bring back memories of my life and of my personal struggle. It is a struggle not just for me, but for the civil rights of others. The words remind me of a people who came over the rough side of the mountain; whose lives were frothed with fear and death and violence and hope. I know of the struggle they describe. I know of the praise and thanksgiving they command. I know of their promise. Will those young ears who hear my words understand as well? Will it have the same meaning for them that it does for me?

I could never improve on the work of James Weldon Johnson, but I can pay tribute to this great musical work composed in the early 1900's by keeping its meaning alive. I can make these words have new life for a generation so far removed from the time they were penned and set to music.

"Lift Every Voice and Sing"

Lift every voice and sing, till earth and Heaven ring,
Ring with the harmonies of liberty;
Let our rejoicing rise, high as the listening skies,
Let it resound loud as the rolling sea.
Sing a song full of the faith that the dark past has taught us,
Sing a song full of the hope that the present has brought us;
Facing the rising sun of our new day begun,
Let us march on till victory is won.

Stony the road we trod, bitter the chastening rod,
Felt in the days when hope unborn had died;
Yet with a steady beat, have not our weary feet,
Come to the place for which our fathers sighed?
We have come over a way that with tears has been watered,
We have come, treading our path through the blood of the slaughtered;
Out from the gloomy past, till now we stand at last
Where the white gleam of our bright star is cast.

God of our weary years, God of our silent tears,
Thou Who hast brought us thus far on the way;
Thou Who hast by Thy might, led us into the light,
Keep us forever in the path, we pray.

Lest our feet stray from the places, our God, where we met Thee.
Lest our hearts, drunk with the wine of the world, we forget Thee.
Shadowed beneath Thy hand, may we forever stand,
True to our God, true to our native land.

Oomph! Oomph! Oomph! Stony the road we trod. Those words take me back and paint a picture in the recesses of my mind of the very roads I traveled, the people I encountered and the change we sought to bring to this ailing and divided nation. They make me remember my own journey. It is not unlike the course of legions of other blacks who grew up in my time. What makes my story so unique is the fact that I was witness to many of the nation's most historic moments. I was there and quite frequently saw cruel injustices made right. And yes – some of it was my doing, my hand that intervened, my voice that called the injustice by name and my God who was there to protect me through it all. I endured berating and beatings. I stood face to face with the Ku Klux Klan and I bear witness to the power of the human spirit. I was determined to make a way out of no way.

SHARECROPPING
NEAR GOULD, ARKANSAS

"Usually, when people talk about the "strength" of black women...they ignore the reality to be strong in the face of oppression is not the same as overcoming oppression, that endurance is not to be confused with transformation."
– Bell Hooks

If I close my eyes and think hard enough, I can hear her voice calling through-out our small four-room ramshackle house. "Time to get up! Time to welcome a new day!"

My mother, Lula Belle Sutton was a giant of a woman, in looks, thoughts, words and deeds. Although she was only educated through the fifth grade, she was the smartest woman I've ever known. She was tall for a woman of that time, stand-ing five-feet nine. Her light-colored skin resembled the color of milk after it kissed a warm cup of coffee on a cool fall day. It had a natural glisten. Her piercing large brown eyes resembled fine gemstones polished and faceted to reflect light as it danced across the surface. She was beauty, whether she was just waking in the morning or retiring after the setting sun. Her persona could light up a room and she was strong of will. She was strength...hardened by the times and events that raised her, calloused by the harshness of those who considered people of color as little more than chattel. Despite her inner pain, Lula Belle managed to display a beautiful façade. She was always magnificently attired and could create a dress from a bolt of cloth in no time at all. In our eyes she was larger than life. She was our provider and all that we ever really knew as a parent. We rarely talked about my father who died when I was about three years old. I'm told he was killed in a farming accident, even though I have never asked for details of his passing. As far as I was concerned, Lula Belle Sutton was father, mother, and sometimes judge, jury and executioner. This tenderhearted woman was a strong disciplinarian and did not have time for children who would misbehave. If Lula Belle said, "Come here!" She meant right now and not five minutes later. She ruled the family with an uncommon strength and love, and we were not about to upset her or the peace and tranquility of our home. Life was Lula Belle's teacher. Pain was her lesson.

Strength was her Savior. Lula Belle's belief in God and self, made her a survivor even amid the tumultuous times of the 1930s.

The cities of the world were recovering from "The Great Depression". The town of Gould, Arkansas is about three miles from the large plantation in Lincoln County where we lived. We managed to survive in a tin-roofed clapboard house right smack dab in the middle of the plantation. The house was so tattered that it appeared that a strong wind might strip it bare leaving only the shallow stone underpinnings and a skeleton of boards that once held up walls. The roof was the best part of the house – but only when it rained. You see there is nothing like the sound of raindrops pelting a tin roof. It starts as a small series of light taps and pings and then the Arkansas sky will open up and deliver a symphony of rhythms in a cadence that will never be duplicated. A gentle and steady rain on the other hand would give you a smooth patter that could easily lull even the most discontent baby into a peaceful long sleep.

There were no trees for shade near the house. The southern sun was relentless and nearly skin scorching. The heat of the day began just as soon as the sun touched the sky and it remained until the orange glow left after its setting. As a small child, it seemed that as far as you could see there was open land to be farmed. In those days as soon as you could walk and listen and take instruction, you were given chores. Everybody in the family worked.

Other sharecropper houses dotted the horizon and the dusty unpaved roads that led from one house to another. Corn cribs and barns were the biggest structures on the landscape. The time of year could be determined by more than just the sights and sounds; it could be deciphered by the smells. The rich soil had a thick and distinctive smell of its own when it was freshly tilled in the spring. The noonday heat beating down on the earth followed by a quick rain shower perfumed the air with yet another aroma. And in the fall the burning leaves and fires that kept the small houses warm were a clear indication that winter was not far away.

We were among several families sharecropping right there on the Holthoff plantation. We needed very few store-bought items because we grew most of our food. Fresh vegetables were a staple and on some nights, a meal. Life was hard. We toiled from sunup to sundown and never gave it a second thought. That was the way it was. We realized that and we fell into place wherever Lula Belle said. We always had our meals as a family and not a morsel was touched without the bowing of heads and the saying of a blessing over the food. It was these rituals of hard work, family food and prayer that kept us together as a unit over the years. We were each other's friend and support. We feared the mighty and omnipotent and gracious God and we thanked him for his blessings, and we adhered to his words and commandments.

Lula Belle Sutton was a tough woman who embraced hard work and insisted the same from her eight children. The early 30's was a time of uncertainty for people of color in rural Arkansas. We were hard worked, impoverished and always lived amid the specter of violent racism. Stories of it somehow managed to trickle all the way down here, though there was no phone, just an across-the-fence conversation. Although the town of Gould was only three long miles from the plantation, it seemed much further, especially when you went there on foot or in a horse drawn wagon. We walked it many-a-time.

Lula Belle's children were her farm hands. We tilled the soil, planted the crops, tended them, and harvested what we could. We picked the cotton and took it to the market. Along the way and throughout life in this rural, sometimes dusty area – we would encounter all kinds of people, both black and white. Just like today, there were good and kind white people but there were just as many who treated us as less than second class citizens. As long as we stayed in "our place", no harm would come to us and we knew how to avoid trouble.

There were two girls and six boys in my family. Lettice Mae was the oldest and there was my sister Delma Lois, the youngest of us all. Like bookends, the girls framed the six boys including Charlie Howard, followed by Samuel, Willie David, Henry L., Olee and then me, the baby boy - Ozell.

My mother had a bedroom, my two sisters had a room and my five brothers and I shared the same room. There was a bed on every wall of our room. Space was limited; love was abundant and as long as we were all together, everything was right with the world; our world. If there is nothing else that I learned from my mother, it was that one must first put faith in God followed by an unmeasured love for family and hard work - no matter your calling.

Lula Belle's love of her children would not allow her to raise them like other children of my era. There had to be something better for each of us. Lula Belle and her children were nurtured through the teachings of a God whose hand was ever present and whose life examples would become ours. We knew God watched over us. We knew we were raised up in prayer by my momma every night as she bent her knees at the side of her bed and whispered her petitions for the basics in life; for her and her brood of children and our extended family – known and unknown.

On Sunday mornings, we would attend church services. No questions, no debate, no arguments. When the sun rose on Sunday, we began the ritual of preparing ourselves for worship. Faces were washed, clothes had been laid out and pressed the night before, shoes were buffed to a shine and minds were cleared of the

11

worries of the week. Our family, like other families who lived around us, had a strong belief that our help came from the power of the Almighty. Our faith caused celebration when things were good and celebration when things were bad. In all things, we offered praise. I was raised poor as Job's turkey, but I was cultured in the wisdom and lessons of the Holy Bible and the church. The teachings are etched on my mind like a scribe wrote them there.

We did not have a regular Sunday preacher. There was a small clapboard rickety church, not much in size to speak of, but it was God's house. We would get a preacher once a month. Ministers were in short supply and would travel from one church to another, sometimes conducting several services in one day. Sometimes on foot, we would follow the preachers from church to church down those dusty back roads, so we could participate in services somewhere on Sunday. I enjoyed attending church, not just for the word, but for the eloquence with which it was delivered. There was nothing like a country preacher and country deacon. When these men opened their mouths to speak, you could feel their words in the cadence and rhythm and the timbre of their voices. Each was different, but they all had a similar message. It was a message of heartfelt thanks to a mighty God who could make a way out of no way. The Church was the place where the worries and cares of the week were released into the hands of a mighty power. The deacon would get it all started by calling everyone to worship. After this, a man would grab an old cane back chair and place it in the front of the church right at center aisle. The man would drop down on one knee, clasp his hands and rest his elbows on the seat of that rickety little chair and there in that clapboard church he would summon up a prayer from the depths of his being. A typical prayer might go something like this:

> *"Heavenly Father, It is once now and again that your humble servants come head bowed and body bent, thanking you Lord for allowing us to gather here just one more time. I want to thank you father for you reached down with a finger of love and you touched me as I slumber, and I slept; and you opened my eyes so that I could see one more day. You put a song in my heart and a prayer on my lips. Heavenly Father, I want to thank you that you didn't make my bed my cooling board; nor my "kiver" my winding sheet. You clothed me in my right mind. You put food on my table and a roof over my head."*

By this time the church members would awaken by shouting, "Un – Huh" or "Amen – Amen" or "Pray brother, Pray".

The cadence with which the prayer was delivered was almost like a song. Its poetic rhythm had a sway to it like a sonnet that caused the mind to see the words and the meaning behind them, just like the lyrics to a hymn. The relatively quiet church would almost instantly begin to rock with the tapping of feet and the lifting of spirits. We had no grand organ. There were no pipes reaching toward the ceiling, and sometimes there wasn't a piano; just the clapping of hands, the tapping of feet and those voices. The sounds would flow through open windows and across fields and fall on the ears of anyone within a few hundred yards. They knew church was in session and that prayers were being sent up. Then those incredible rolling voices that would hit notes so high, or so low, you could almost feel the vibrations on the surface of your skin. To me some of the most powerful music was created when no instruments played. Deep in their soul these magnificent beings would summon up a voice that could soothe pains, lift spirits or rock the house. The songs spoke of the harshness of life and the promise of a better day. The songs themselves were almost like prayers set to music.

Oh yes, fix me, Jesus, fix me.
Fix me so that I can walk on
a little while longer.
Fix me so that I can pray on
just a little bit harder.
Fix me so that I can sing on
just a little bit louder.
Fix me so that I can go on despite the pain,
The fear, the doubt, and yes, the anger,
I ask not that you take this cross from me,
only that you give me the strength to continue carrying it onward
'til my dying day.
Oh, fix me, Jesus, fix me.

It was this faith that people had to rely on. They had nothing else. There was no real promise of things getting better except for the promise given to us in the scriptures.

<u>Joshua 1:5</u>
No one will be able to stand up against you all the days of your life. As I was with Moses, so I will be with you; I will never leave you nor forsake you.

1 Kings 11:38

If you do whatever I command you and walk in my ways and do what is right in my eyes by keeping my statutes and commands, as David my servant did, I will be with you. I will build you a dynasty as enduring as the one I built for David and will give Israel to you.

2 Thessalonians 3:3

But the Lord is faithful, and he will strengthen and protect you from the evil one.

Many of the people of that day could not read, but they knew scriptures. They could not read music, but they knew how to make a melody. They could not write a speech or a sermon, but they could speak from the heart and testify about the goodness of their God. This is the testament to faith that our people relied on. It was the power of the church and leadership of stalwart Christians who led the way from slavery, to freedom, through the oppressive days in the sometimes cruel south through the civil rights movement and now to future lives. It is that faith in the unseen that powered the powerless and gave sound to those who had no voice. Again and again, we put stock in the faith and the lessons of our God.

> *"Then the disciples came to Jesus privately and said, "Why could we not cast it out?" He said to them, 'Because of your little faith. For truly I tell you, if you have faith the size of a mustard seed, you will say to this mountain, 'Move from here to there,' and it will move; and nothing will be impossible for you."*
> – Matthew 17: 19-20

In her own way Lula Belle tried to prepare us to deal with the harshness of the times and the realities of surviving it all. She had an abiding faith that she passed on to us. Although she was not an educated woman, Lula Belle was quite a teacher. She drilled into us lessons in life that would be a comfort and a help in some troubling times. She taught us to love everybody and to always be of service. I can remember very vividly having her stand face to face with me and saying:

"....Look up to no man....Look down on none...Look every man straight in the eye as a brother....as an equal."

My mother stressed education for her children. All it took was for her to glance at her surroundings and then into the faces of her children to know that there had to be a better life for them. In each of our faces she could see the future and she knew that future was not here. It was somewhere else. It was far away from this rickety old house and the near slavery mentality that kept us here. No, if she had anything to do with it, she would represent the last generation of the unlearned and uneducated. Her offspring would be those who would be leaders and educators, but most of all they would be good people.

I remember standing many a night as she sat in a chair, bone weary from a day of labor and I recited Paul Lawrence Dunbar and Langston Hughes. She loved Dunbar's prose. It was as if he was writing for her, about her and about her condition. Dunbar only lived to be 33 years old, but somehow he mastered two languages. The Dayton, Ohio native wrote short stories, novels, plays, songs and essays in the voice of Standard English and in the turn-of-the century black dialect of that time. And of course, Hughes wrote one poem in particular that I always liken to Lula Belle. I would recite it and she would think it was written for her. The words capture the sentiment of how she was able to rear these boys and girls in the most troubling of times.

By the light of a crackling fire and the dimness of the room, I stood ready to recite. Her face careworn from a hard day's work was yet still strikingly beautiful. Her eyelids would close slightly and her head would tilt back as I launched into her favorite poem:

Mother to Son
By Langston Hughes

Well, son, I'll tell you:
Life for me ain't been no crystal stair.
It's had tacks in it,
And splinters
And boards torn up,
An places with no carpet on the floor –
Bare.
But all the time
I'se been a-climbin' on,
And reachin' landins'
And turnin' corners,
And sometimes goin' in the dark
Where there ain't been no light.
So, boy, don't you turn back.

15

Don't you set down on the steps.
'Cause you finds it kinder hard.
Don't you fall now –
For I'se still goin', honey,
I'se still climbin,
And life for me ain't been no crystal stair.

When the final words were uttered, she'd pull me tight and gently kiss my forehead and thank me and off we'd go to our rooms for some much needed sleep. Another workday was just hours away.

We moved many times during my growing up years. We were always searching for the better life and opportunities. For the most part that simply did not exist in rural Arkansas for Negroes. We were presented with new and old challenges each time we moved. We moved once from one farm to another. We went to work and live on the property owned by Mr. Claude Holthoff. It was hard to earn any money at all on that farm.

As far as I was concerned, sharecropping was only a step or two away from slavery. I never knew anyone who became rich from working the fields and then giving up almost half your crop to the man who owns the land. The owners were the ones who made most of the money. They were wealthy to begin with and then took on poor people who had no where else to go as their farm workers.

The money was sparse and the work was extremely hard. I remember vividly a disagreement my mother had with old man Holthoff.

As sharecroppers, we tended about 40 acres. Holthoff owned hundreds of acres of land at this plantation. Mr. Holthoff was a brusque man, sharp-tongued and short-tempered. I don't recall ever hearing a kind word from him. His concern was only about the money. He was demanding of the people who share cropped his land and he had no room for excuses, only results at harvest. That is what he understood; this is what he demanded.

Our money was so tied up in the plantation until many times we owed more money than we made. Every sharecropper had what was known as a draw – a line of credit. We had incurred expenses from that line of credit to buy seed, fertilizer and everything we needed to produce a crop. As you might guess, many times the land owner also owned the feed store, general store and anything else we needed. At the end of the year, we did all the work. But the plantation owner got his half, or more than half, and we had to pay the bill on the line of credit. That was usually more than half of our indebtedness. So the plantation owner has us two ways. Our debt would be heavy because ol' man Holthoff charged more than what would be normal and the interest rate was an usury level. My mother was pretty good with numbers and was certain when she sent my older brother, Charlie, to sell our family's last bale of cotton, it would be pure profit. She would be out of debt and was ready to collect on her season of hard work.

Now you have to know that a bale of cotton is no small thing. It weighs almost 500 pounds and took days to pick and bale. So mama sent Charlie into town with what she knew was going to be her "cash crop". It had been a good harvest in 1937. Before Charlie could make the sale he was stopped by the plantation owner.

"Charlie, you can't sell that bale of cotton. Your mother still owes me money!" Charlie being obedient didn't want to argue with the man. In those days a simple disagreement could escalate into something more serious. Charlie was not about to get into a verbal sparring with this white man to whom his mother had paid so much.

Charlie did the only thing he could in that situation. He left the bale of cotton right there and hustled back home to his mother. Lula Belle had just washed her hair and was not ready to leave the house when she learned the news of the dispute. However, she simply wrapped her wet hair up and she took off on foot walking briskly – almost like soldiers going to war – with all her eight children in tow.

It was nothing for us to walk the three miles to town. We lived a mile down a dirt road which led to a pike –gravel road. We were almost running to keep pace with momma who was marching as if to war. The moments that followed proved that statement to be nearly true. Lula Belle clearly had a plan to get her last bale of cotton or her money before she returned home. We were anxious to see how she was going to do that.

With a look of determination in her eyes, she stormed into the store. She walked right up past everyone else in the place to position herself just inches away from the face of ol man Holthoff and shouted, "What's this business about owing you some money?"

Mr. Holthoff replies, "You are not out of debt."

Mama tapped her foot on the floor and says, "I am out of debt." The volume continued to increase and the verbal sparring was on. In the exchange of accusations and counter remarks - some harsh words zipped about and hung in the air like flies over honey. That was the first time I heard my mother curse. After all, she was a very faithful sister in the Baptist church, but these words came with an ease and fury that told me this was not the first time they had crossed momma's lips.

17

"Lula Belle, are you calling me a liar?" Mr. Holthoff said. And that is something you didn't do to a white person in those times.

"You damn right you are a liar and I want my cotton," Mama replied.

Well that brought everything to a standstill. Nobody moved and it was clear that this was going nowhere fast.

Lula Belle wheeled around told my older brother to go ask Uncle Gus could she borrow his wagon, but not to tell Gus what the problem was because he would come up there and get into bigger trouble. After all, Uncle Gus was 6 feet 6 inches and 240 pounds and was known for sparking a quick temper, if provoked. She did not want Uncle Gus to get mixed up in the situation. The store was full of mostly black people and a few whites. The blacks in the store tried to get mama out of the store. She refused to leave. But instead, they left the store and stood outside peeping through the windows. That left the Holthoff family and the Sutton family staring at each other, remaining in the store. I would be much older before I would understand this strategy. Now as I said this bale of cotton weighed about 500 pounds. In pretty short order my brother returned with Uncle Gus' wagon.

Mr. Holthoff stood between mama and the cotton, trying to block her way. He shouted, "Don't touch that cotton!"

My brothers heard the words but didn't pay the ol' man any mind. They answered to a much tougher authority, their mama. They yanked up that bale of cotton like it weighed nothing at all. They threw it on the wagon and we rode off with the cotton and the memory of what had just transpired etched in our minds. And there Mr. Holthoff stood, speechless, as we disappeared beyond the horizon and into the cloud kicked up on that dusty road. We went looking for another place to sell that cotton.

Well after that we had to leave the farm.

As we rode away, I relived what I had just seen and I pondered the actions of this woman we called momma. I realized that I had just learned a valuable lesson from that experience. I learned that a man or woman has to stand for that in which he or she believes, no matter what the possible cost. I learned that sometimes in life you work extremely hard to get something and others will try to take it away from you. Most importantly though, I learned that with determination there comes resolve and at the end of the day no matter the outcome, you have the pride in knowing you were steadfast in your belief. That situation back on the farm could have bought my mama and her children a serious beating or worse. Fear never crept into Lula Belle's eyes. She stood tall and never took her gaze off her target. She knew that her circumstances were of the Lord's doing and that he would protect and provide. Lula

Belle showed me and my siblings how to stand up in the face of adversity and how to hide my fear.

Years later in my life, I would see how this incident would come full circle to me. Not everyone involved would remember what happened that hot day, but I didn't forget. I would never forget it. After that day we began the search for a new home and more work to sustain us. There simply was no way around it. My mother was not worried and knew we would find something suitable for our family. The Lord always provided.

We moved into the town of Gould. When we got there we became day laborers with the exception of mama and my younger sister. My older sister had gone to stay with an aunt in St. Louis to attend high school because there was not a high school for blacks to attend in Gould. For blacks, school stopped after the eighth grade. So, it was mama, her boys and the younger daughter. By that time, my older brother had a separate family who lived in Grady. We worked on the various big farms around Gould. In the day laboring business, we would board a truck into town before daylight, and we would load up on that truck, waiting to be chosen for work at home improvement stores. The truck would come in before daylight to the big cotton farms, which were near the Arkansas River.

As soon as daylight would appear, we would already be in position in the fields to start chopping or picking. If we were chopping, it was spring. If we were picking, it was the fall. Planting and cultivating in the spring and reaping in the fall. There were three groups of workers, the black hands, prisoners, who were mostly black, and Hispanic itinerant workers. We would be in different sections. We liked to say that we picked from, "kin to kin't," or better yet, can to can't. That means from the time you can see to the time you can't see. We received $1 a day. We talked and sometimes we sang. Our fingers would get sore and the cotton buds would cause your hands to bleed. Our group consisted of about 30.

The man would always hire a leader, called a lead-row man. He was paid 10 cents more than everybody else to keep the chopping pace. He was usually a mature black man who was experienced and could usually chop faster than the average person. One particular day, the young folk grew aggravated that the lead-row was setting the pace at a rate that was faster than the older people could keep up with. If the overseer noticed that the older people slowed down the progress, they would not be allowed to come back. And these people sorely needed the work. They had families and children to feed on the meager dollars they brought in from this backbreaking work.

We were mad at the lead-row man. So, we decided to take him on. I would take the row beside him. Because when you were chopping cotton you are actually chopping the row next to where the person on the next row is standing and you are slightly behind them. "We would say, "You better move old man or you will get your leg chopped." We would drive him hard. I would fall back and at the end of the row, we would switch and let somebody else take him on. One of us had him going at full speed all the time. One day about three o'clock in the afternoon, he got too hot. To make matters more difficult for the lead-row, the water boy would make sure everybody got a drink of water from the dipper that they all shared before the lead row and if any water was left in the bucket, he would pour it out before it got to him. The lead-row man got too hot and had to go to seek comfort in the shade of a big tree. He collapsed there for a while trying to catch his breath – all the while keeping his eyes peeled for the overseer. The last thing he wanted was his supervisor to catch him resting while everyone else was in the sun working. We laughed so hard that day. The 13, 14 and 15-year-olds were taking him on. We said, "Alright old man you could start your mess again if you want, but we will kill you. We will work you 'til you drop right there in the middle of the field" It has been my life to watch black folks take on obstacles and make it. The lead-row was an obstacle. We did not do this for ourselves, but we did this for others. It was in a sense a foreshadowing of what I would do in the years to come. I would fight for the underdog, oppressed, mistreated and forgotten people. A little boy in the middle of a hot field under the Arkansas sun was setting the stage for some great things – one thing at a time. My actions would likely have never been seen by anyone. My intent was to be the burr in the saddle that makes a horse jump and jolt until someone came to remove the irritation – to make things right. I realized I could do great things and I would never be alone.

"FACING THE RISING SUN OF OUR NEW DAY BEGUN…"

The program at the Douglass High School is moving along well. It's a grand day for the young people. I will have to do extremely well to etch in their memory the message I will deliver. The good thing is that James Weldon Johnson has done much of the work for me. You have to wonder what was going on in his life to pen the words of the Negro National Anthem in such a way that the words and their meaning would transcend time. The words become more precious to me as time goes by.

> *Lift every voice and sing, till earth and Heaven ring,*
> *Ring with the harmonies of liberty;*
> *Let our rejoicing rise, high as the listening skies,*
> *Let it resound loud as the rolling sea.*
> *Sing a song full of the faith that the dark past has taught us,*
> *Sing a song full of the hope that the present has brought us;*
> *Facing the rising sun of our new day begun,*
> *Let us march on till victory is won.*

The two lines in the middle of the song are so striking.

> *Sing a song full of the faith that the dark past has taught us,*
> *Sing a song full of the hope that the present has brought us*

At the time I was growing up, I never thought about my life as having a dark past. I always believed that for the circumstances, the love of family and the closeness we shared overshadowed anything bad in our lives and in the lives of other black people living in the Deep South. Maybe we concentrated more on the next line – a song full of hope.

I have never belittled the analysis of my life. It was hard. It was damned hard and the future was never certain. It was unclear what would happen next to us, good or bad. We took life as it came – one day at a time. But we had hope. We had faith and we had a mother who kept us focused on the here and now with a keen eye toward the future. Lula Belle knew for us to overcome our circumstance, we would have to be educated. We were smart, but we needed to have formal training and to one day leave the area in search of greater opportunity. But in a flash of seconds, my pursuit of learning would come to a screeching halt.

The summer months always seemed to go by very quickly. We had long hard days, but we worked from sunup to sundown so the hours seemed to fly by sometimes. On our land we had to provide for the main farm and provide some things for ourselves. Long before winter came, we would have to plan for the meals when fresh vegetables were not available. On our property, which was really the plantation owner's property, we grew corn, peas and other vegetables for family consumption. There were two things that were absolutely essential for the winter.

First, we needed roughly thirty to forty gallons of molasses. We had to grow the cane. It had to be stripped and then ground to produce the juices. We cooked all day in large cast iron pots over an open flame. The end result was a dark sweet syrup, molasses. This substance would be mighty tasty in the winter months. We put it on hot buttered cornbread or gigantic lighter-than-air-biscuits. It was also used in baking – to make cakes and pies.

I would feed the cane into the mill. A horse would walk around in a circle – tied to a post that was connected to a large stone wheel with cogs – and connected to another wheel and eventually to the pressing stones. You had to pay attention to what you were doing. If you fed the cane in there and did not pull your hand back, it most surely would be caught and you could lose your hand. At my age though, this was about the safest task I ever had.

For the winter months, we needed roughly 400 pounds of salt pork. We kept everything. No part of the hog was thrown away. We would even keep the hoofs. The hoofs were used to make a very strong tea as a remedy for a cold. We would tend to those hogs with a special care, feeding them – making sure they had enough water. These animals would sustain us in the toughest of times; in the coldest of weather. A loss in livestock could be the difference between having enough to eat and having little or nothing at all.

The first frost of the winter would be a significant sign for everyone on the farm in those days. The icy morning crystals that covered everything in sight would signal the end of the growing season. Crunching underfoot, the frost would give a glisten to the morning, especially when the sun first touched the sky. This thin layer of ice would disappear almost as quickly and as quietly as it came. The result of this act of nature would damage tender plants and render them useless. But to the hog farmer this frost would mean much more. It's time for hog killing.

Not far from our house lived my mother's brother, Uncle Gus – a giant of a man who had 9 boys and one girl. They lived as we lived, at the mercy of the plantation owner. We lived by the owner's rules and did all we could to care for ourselves. Uncle Gus was in charge of the hog killings. His boys and my brothers and I followed his orders. Uncle Gus' experience ensured we could maximize our yield from the hog. There was good eating from a full grown hog and a single mistake could mean a waste of food, something we could ill afford. For some, the details of a hog killing are just too hard to imagine, but suffice to say that every step was necessary.

Because of the sheer weight of the hog, we needed an army of men. On hog killing day, we could take down as many as 15 – 20 hogs. Several families would sometimes work together and share the load. Women would get the cut down pieces and make sausage or start to cure the hams.

Long before that process, the animal is killed and the big parts are prepared. Among the most dangerous parts of this process is removing the hair from the pig. Scalding hot water was used to loosen the hair that was scraped loose leaving a smooth outer skin. Large pots would sit on the open fire. The water was set to boil long before the first hog was killed and throughout the morning, more would be added as quickly as it was used.

One morning my brothers were carrying the water in wooden pails. Scalding hot water caused steam to rise into the cold morning air. The bale on my brother's bucket broke just at the same time that he was passing by me. The water sloshed everywhere and poured down my right leg. Scalding hot water. I rolled around on the ground in pain. I could feel the skin blister and become raw – bare – open to the pain that seared right to the bone. My brothers carried me to the house where my mother went to work. There was no doctor to call. There was no emergency room to run to. All we had was our country ways and our own remedies. My mother would care for me over a period of months. I missed a whole year of school and tried to learn what I could while at home. When my mother was able to scrape up a few dollars, she took me to the doctor. He was amazed that I was even alive. Mother had cared for my wounds using country medicine and I was on my way to recovery. It was difficult for me to miss school. I loved learning and would foster that love for the rest of my life. I romanced the fact that once I learned something, it was mine. Mine, as long I held on to it, and used the knowledge I stored. In the days to come, I would be forced to call upon those lessons I learned in my childhood. Over and over again, I would have to remember the words of my mother and everyone who touched my life along the journey. The days ahead would be dedicated to making things right and touching the lives of others and continuing to learn. There would be stumbling blocks and people who would try to hold me back, but just like that tree planted by the waters, "I shall not be moved."

My early learning was in a one room school with one teacher for all of the black children in my area. For grades one through eight, I walked some three miles to the colored school. We dared not be late – for there was a price to pay. Corporal punishment was real and dealt out without hesitation. In those days most all of the children were raised on a farm. Farming came first. As a result blacks only went to school seven months a year because the chores on the plantation had to continue and the children – some as young as six or seven had to perform those tasks. All of us were sharecroppers and we knew that come harvest time – there could be no school. We were at the mercy of the weather. The crops had to be gathered when the weather permitted and before they rotted in the field. Some of the crops had to be processed – dried and prepared for storage. All this took time and all hands were required. Our school calendar year never matched the calendar of white students in all white schools. We started our schooling in September. But by then white kids had already been in class for months.

I always said that the white man wanted to declare me inferior and tried to make good on that by giving me an inferior education and less access to opportunity. But they didn't know my mama, Lula Belle never allowed me to address a single notion of being inferior. She would always say, "Boy you are as good as the next boy."

"Boy you are as good as any and better than none." So I grew up with the notion that I am no better than anyone. "Look every man in the eye and treat him as an equal" was her mantra. It became the basis of my existence and the foundation of my thinking. Those wise words came from the lips of a woman who only had a fifth grade education. She expected more out of us in the seven months we were in school than white students did in nine. As a result, I grew up thinking my education was just as good as any.

I learned pretty early the advantages of education. If I was busy learning something or reading, I would not have to perform chores. Mama would say, "Leave that boy alone, can't you see he's reading?"

For the first three grades of my education, I attended a one-room school. One teacher was responsible for all of us. The older children sometimes helped with the smaller ones. It was amazing some of the things you learned in that day and not everything you learned was part of the traditional lessons and studies. Our teacher was concerned about the whole person, mind, body, and spirit. I learned early on the importance of caring for my body. Our teacher wanted everyone to be clean and pressed when you arrived at her one-room school. One of the first things she would do is line everyone up and have them hold out their hands. She would walk around the room, up and down the line inspecting the hands. She wanted every-one to have clean hands and clean nails. If she spotted a speck of dirt, she would rap you across the dirty hand with a short stick. It only took one time for me to be standing there rubbing my stinging knuckles to learn not to come to school with dirty hands. As a result, I would volunteer to wash the breakfast dishes before I left home for school. That way I could kill two birds with one stone. Clean dishes; clean hands.

After the third grade, we walked quite a distance to the "colored school" in the town of Gould. My sister and I would walk together. Rain or shine, cold or hot, we would be out there walking every day. Each of those days a school bus carrying the white children would pass sometimes splashing water and snow all over us. One day I had been particularly upset about being passed by the bus that was going right past our school. That night I asked my mama, "Why does the bus pass us by?"

Lula Belle let the words sink in, but soon answered. "Son, there is no good reason for the bus not stopping to pick you up. It's just the way it is." Although she was tough as nails, I now know this must have been painful for her to say. I know she wanted the best for her children, but she also was keenly aware of the time in which we lived. No black children we knew of ever rode the school bus. We all walked. Some were even taunted by the kids as they rode by. Often they would throw things or shout bad names as they sat in the comfort of that bus. Lula Belle knew she could not protect us from the truth, so that is what she told us - the truth, no matter how painful. This was adequate preparation for the future. We may not have fully understood, and Lula Belle was not about to rationalize the merits of our reality. At the same time she professed her children were as good as anybody's. We were as beautiful as anybody's. We were as smart as any other child. She was partly resigned to the fact that this is the way things would be and would remain. I on the other hand had other ideas. In my own stubborn way, I would take the praise of Lula Belle and take it a step further. I wanted to put my ideas and my thoughts into action and to bring about change. There was no rational reason in my thinking for the way we were treated. I could envision my rebellion of "the system" in my future. Wait, just wait till I get the chance. My time is coming.

After thinking about what my mother said about the bus passing us by, I told her, "When I grow up, my children will not be treated like that. They will ride the bus!"

Lula Belle chuckled and skeptically said, "Ozell, what are you going to do about it?"

"I don't know, but things are going to be better." I said it, and even at that early age, I believed it. I believed I could do anything. After all, Lula Belle said "You're as good as anybody!"

Even without the admonishment of Lula Belle, I was determined to be a good student and to perform well in anything I chose to do. I loved and respect the work and challenge of having lived on a farm. It is the backbone of America, the foundation of our people, providing food and plant products for the benefit of all. However, I knew there was an opportunity for me to be of service to people. I could not stand to watch the vestiges of racism and hatred and not do anything about it. Education would be my vehicle to serve others. I would endure my own struggles while trying to make a life for myself and for my family. First though, I had to get a diploma – the piece of paper that says to everyone I am accomplished at learning. Little did I know that even the most degreed black man would not get the respect due him. It was however a beginning. If nothing more than for self gratification and for propping up my own ego, I knew that books and classrooms would give me insight and answers and ideas to all of my life's questions.

The Gould Colored School took pupils through the eighth grade. In order to continue through high school, I would have to go to all the way to Little Rock, about 80 miles north of Gould. I performed well at school. I was at the head of my class and only days away from graduating. I was the valedictorian of the class. I had written my speech and had practiced it to perfection.

Friends and Graduates, this is the end of the school year. The end of the last day, the end of the program, but it is not the end of our ambition. It is just the beginning!

Now that we have been shown the paths to real happiness, we are determined to never follow another. No way – no matter how enticing it may look – will be able to lead us away from the road to real work; the road to education.

We know not where other roads lead nor where they end, but our years of working and studying have proven to us that the one we are on now will lead us to a land of unending riches and wealth.

The greatest glory is ours today we realize, but there are others who must share in that glory – our parents and our teachers. Where would we be without the unending support of them both? With the support of the former and the latter, we have achieved where we might have failed. We have won

*when we might have lost. Now we are going on to higher
educational opportunities – to high schools and to college –
but we will not forget the place where we got our start.*

It has been sixty years since I wrote that. I remember every word and remember every feeling of each sentence. The sad thing though, is that I never got to deliver that graduation address.

My brother had come by the house on the day of graduation to tell me he had found work for me. I would have to leave right away. Jobs were hard to come by for blacks in those days so any opportunity to make money outside of farming was cherished. I had to go. I had to take this job. I would be working long hours at night washing dishes at a local restaurant.

This had to be the most depressing day of my young life. While I was there in that kitchen surrounded by pots and pans and an endless supply of dirty dishes, my friends were graduating and no doubt, someone else was standing in my place and delivering a message to the graduates and their loved one. The other workers at the restaurant knew something was bothering me. They could detect my sadness and my disappointment, but I tried to be strong and to deny my pain. I insisted that I was alright and that nothing was wrong. I warmed up the water in the giant sink and grabbed another load of dishes from the kitchen and I continued working. Fighting back the tears, I pressed on.

After my shift I grabbed my things and set out for what would no doubt be a long walk home. The path was blurred by the drops of water that formed in my eyes. I kept my head low so that anyone passing me could not witness the tears that held their place in the wells of my eyes. Step by step, I shuffled down the street not really wanting to go home, but anxious to get out of sight of everyone. I turned the corner to discover that I was at our little house. When I entered the door it all hit me – a torrent of tears streamed down my face and Lula Belle was right there to wipe each one away. She held me tight for what seemed like hours. She didn't try to tell me it would be alright; instead she let me cry and have my moment of grief. She let me handle this on my terms and I could swear she was crying too, feeling sorrow for her baby boy. Soon my crying would be over and Lula Belle's strength would become my strength. I would once again hold my head high and realize that with life there comes disappointment for which there is no immediate cure.

The speech I penned did not go to waste. I would be invited back years later to Gould to speak for commencement. I finally gave my address and while talking that day, I remembered with distinct clarity what had happened years before. I had spoken many times at various venues, but this was special beyond measure. I could barely hold back the tears – remembering the struggle I had endured for the opportunity to stand there and speak for my own graduation. I was forced to imagine what the room would have looked like, guessed at where my family would have been sitting and pondered the response to my words had I been there the night of my graduation. The delayed gratification was still sweet and no doubt in my mind that part of my journey was now complete.

When I moved to Little Rock, I moved in with my older brother. A short time later, my mother and sister moved there. We got two rooms in a very large rooming house. Mother could not afford a home of her own, but she would make do with what she could until she could do better. For now this rooming house was it. We could live here until we had the opportunity to move into a house. We were no strangers to moving. Times were hard and there were many moves in my lifetime. It seemed that every time the rent was due, we moved.

We were in that big rooming house with a number of other families, who also were looking for inexpensive housing, for the time being. We had the two rooms, a room for me and a room for mother and my sister. Mother was so protective of us, she insisted that she would go down to the one kitchen in the house and cook at night and then bring the food back to our beat-up little rooms. We had a little refrigerator, actually it was no refrigerator – it was an ice box that required a new block of ice every couple of days. So she would bring our meals and there we would stay. She made sure we were separated from the other people in the house. I was in my early teens about this time.

We moved from there to a little house that had four rooms. This house had two bedrooms, one for me and one for my mother and my sister, a living room and a small kitchen. But the lady who owned the place was very possessive. I was washing dishes downtown and got off work at midnight. My mother would leave the porch light on for me to see how to get into the house after my shift. Our electricity was connected to the power for the main house. The lady started complaining about the porch light being on. I remember my mother offering to pay more money to compensate for the additional power at night. She was determined at any cost for the light to be on for her son. The owner of the house confronted my mother about this on more than one occasion and I remember her threatening to whip mama. I think the woman's name was Collier.

Lula Belle looked sternly at the woman, took up a stiff posture and said, "Now Collier, you listen to me because you do not listen very well. Now I told you I would pay you extra money to leave that light on so my son can get in this house safely at night. He works downtown washing dishes and doesn't get off till

28

midnight. Now this light will stay on till he gets home and that is final. Now about you whipping me, well Collier, I will mop up this ground with you. Don't make me act ugly just because you are acting ugly. Because there is no way you are gonna whip me, I will mop up the ground with you! Now I told you I would pay extra and I will, because that light is gonna stay on till my boy gets home."

Mrs. Collier looked dumbfounded. Lula Belle did not move. In just a few short moments, knowing she was painted into a corner, the landlady said in a low meek voice, "Okay, just be sure to pay." The light stayed on. This may seem like a little thing, but it was a major lesson for me. It taught me, as Lula Belle always did, that you have to stand up for that in which you believe. She could have faced eviction for that confrontation, but she didn't. She knew that if anything is important enough, valuable enough, and crucial enough in your life or in the lives of others, you have the obligation to protect it; to stand up and make your voice be heard; and make your resolve clear. Day by day, I learned little lessons from this woman that would continue to prepare me for the life ahead. These little seeds, nuggets of wisdom would prove to be valuable in some rough times. I would recall these lessons, just at the right time and in the proper context, when they were needed the most.

It turned out that about six months later Mama was able to buy a house. My brother, Olee, was already in the military when the war started and then my brother Henry and my brother Sam and my brother David joined the force. They all had made financial allotments to my mother. For some reason their funds had been delayed in coming. Then one day to her surprise she received a lump sum. So she took that money and she got us a house. She lacked a couple hundred dollars to make the full payment, so I borrowed $200 dollars from the man who owned the restaurant where I washed dishes. I paid him back five dollars a week and we were able to buy that house. This home was nothing grand, but it was ours and it would be the place that held some of the greatest memories for me. This home also became the place where other family members from the country would come when they were making their way from the farms and fields to jobs in the city.

You see at this time in history we were experiencing what was known as the second "Great Migration". The first migration started about 1910. Millions of people made the move from the south to the north. They were trying to escape the oppressive climate following slavery that seemed never to end. It was a time of opportunity. African Americans sought a better life and education up north. As a result they would pack up everything they owned and move from the rural areas to the cities. Since there were few hotels where black people could stay and no money – even if there were – so relative's homes became respites on the long journey. Family members and friends would provide shelter and meals as much as they could afford. The first wave as I said started around 1910 and ran till the 1940's. From the 40's to the 70's there was this second wave of movement. Sometimes the pilgrimage was simply from the small towns and farms to a bigger city still in the south. Thus, the tradition of families becoming extended to accommodate blood relatives or friends who were like family.

So in keeping with this tradition people came up and stayed with Mama. One relative lived with us while she attended beauty school. A cousin came and stayed with Mama while he studied at the Arkansas Baptist College to complete his degree in the ministry. She later had my brother David's daughter come to live with us, a child that even my brother did not claim as his own until she lived with Mama. She was very good about taking in those in need because she, herself, had been a person in need. She would lend a hand to everybody she could. She would help total strangers and she would pray for anybody – no matter their dilemma, especially her children. This little house was something special. It held us together as a family. It sheltered us from the harshness of life and became a respite for the weary. In this house, we were grand, if nothing but in a state of mind. Home has always been a wonderful place for me, for its love and protection and the lessons learned from family. This would be important because it was from here that I left my family for the first time, only to be sent thousands of miles away to fight in a war from which many men did not return.

"War – A World Away"

I would like to have said that upon my graduation from high school, I went right into college, but it was not to be. We were a nation at war and at age 18, young men were automatically drafted into the military. I became a marine and was prepared to serve my country and fight if necessary.

World War II was a long and bitter struggle. It began in my early teens and continued until I was 20. I was still in Gould, Arkansas attending the "Gould Colored School" when the United States entered the war in December 1941. I joined millions of other teenagers who were being called into service. I reported for induction into the U.S. Marine Corps in March of 1944. I thought I was headed for the United States Navy and the Naval Base in the Great Lakes. I arose early that day and was prepared to take the oath at the appointed hour. I knew I would make a fine sailor in the United States Navy. It was generally thought by others and by me as well, that the Marines did not draft; and that all inductees were volunteers. So along with several other students from Dunbar High School in Little Rock, I was headed for the Navy, or so I thought.

When the naval officials began calling the roll of inductees that day, they immediately announced the Marines wanted 12 volunteers for induction into the corps. Only six or seven men stepped forward. A marine officer then stated he was going to look through the list of inductees and randomly draw names until he reached his quota. The very first name he pulled from the stack was mine and he yelled, "Ozell Sutton!" I didn't answer. I remained quiet and still, hoping he would move on to the next name. I wanted very badly to go to the Navy with my buddies from Dunbar High School. Again the officer yelled, "Ozell Sutton!" I did not answer. A third time he called. "Is Ozell Sutton here?" I meekly responded, "I am here!" He stamped my papers in a matter of fact way. "You are in the U.S. Marines now." He separated me along with the others who were to go into the U.S.M.C. When the corps had its 12 men, we were gathered, taken to the train station and shipped off to Montford Point, Camp Lejeune, North Carolina.

I had been out of Arkansas only a couple of times to visit older brothers and a sister. They moved to St. Louis in the 1930s in the black exodus from the South. Also, I was accustomed to a school environment and this was far different from anything I had known. I was filled with anxiety and excitement. I entered the Marine Corps when there were only a few blacks. The military was segregated in 1944 and Montford Point was the base where black marines were trained.

31

We trained in the usual segregated way, separate and unequal. We had all white officers and black noncommissioned officers.

As crude and unfair as it was, we were the second wave of black marines. Montford Point was the home of the very first blacks to enter the corps. In 1941, months before Pearl Harbor, the United States was still trying to determine what to do with the blacks who wore the uniforms of the various armed services. It was the insistence of first lady Eleanor Roosevelt who created an opportunity for blacks to be treated more like soldiers and less like the servants of the military. On June 25, 1941, President Franklin Delano Roosevelt signed Executive Order 8802. This act paved the way for blacks to serve on the front lines, to have a means to rise through the ranks and end the level of segregation that existed. The federal government appeared to react slowly to change. But the military seemed to accept change at a snail's pace. President Roosevelt's order would accomplish a number of things for people of color. It would force the full participation of blacks in the military and would require any company with a government contract to also pledge not to discriminate. So now, even nonmilitary blacks would have a chance at a better life. They could hold jobs and earn wages from companies that held large contracts with the U.S. Military. It did not, however, fully desegregate the military. The separate and unequal rule would last for some time to come. It was not until July 1948 that President Harry S. Truman would sign Executive Order 9981. This order totally desegregated the military. However, it was an order not fulfilled until the Secretary of Defense announced an end to segregation on September 30, 1954. During that time, men of all colors would enlist, be trained, fight, and sometimes die on the battlefield for a military and a country that allowed them to be treated as second-class citizens. Change is hard for many people, especially when they fail to recognize people as people. Once again, the words of Lula Belle would ring true in my ears.

"Look up to no man....Look down on no one... Look every man straight in the eye as a brother....As an equal."

The military should have had Lula Belle as a commander.

Montford Point at Camp Lejeune had to be one of the hottest places on earth. It was hot not only because of the incredible temperature and humidity, but also because of the racial climate on the base. Here we were pushed to the westernmost point on this massive base, a clear indication that we were not welcome here. The white U.S. Marines who lived and trained there did so out of our sight, or more accurately, we were out of their sight. Add to that the fact that we lived in metal barracks called Quonset huts. The sun beat down on that metal and the heat of the day was captured inside like a kiln readying to cure clay into pottery.

Nighttime didn't bring any relief either. The thick air of the day seemed equally oppressive at night. There was no movement, no breeze. The air was heavy like a woolen blanket. Clothing would stick to you like a second layer of skin, only this was ponderous and facilitated the beading perspiration. This was coastal North Carolina, with mosquitoes big enough to sap your blood and your strength.

The base was enormous, but Montford Point's accommodations for black marines were not. We were cramped into quarters not fit for human occupation. Leaving the base was rarely an option. There was no escape, no respite, no evasion from the racism on base – because it was even worse for blacks in the nearby segregated town...Jacksonville, North Carolina. Our segment of the base included a headquarters building, a chapel, two warehouses, a mess hall, a dispensary, a steam generating plant, a motor pool, and recreational facilities for the white enlisted men who initially staffed the operation, and of course there was a barber shop.

The 120 green painted prefabricated huts were pushed as far and nestled as close to the western border as possible. Inside those barracks were proud black men who gladly served their country. These Marines would endure the strains of training, the uncertainty of war, and the threat of death at the hands of the enemy. None of it, however would be as humiliating as the treatment received from white soldiers and a country ill prepared to enforce desegregation.

The admission of blacks to the Marines was met with resistance from the other marines and from some of the commanding officers. Blacks were trained by Black noncommissioned officers who were under the leadership of white commanding officers. It was no easy ride under a black trainer. They pushed us harder than the white marines. Our trainers were unrelenting. We worked harder than our white counterparts and when it came down to it, I think we fought just as hard if not harder. Far too frequently, the war was not with the Japanese, it was within the corps. It was White against Black. There were no winners.

I experienced both pride and debasement in the Marine Corps. On one hand, I was extremely proud to enter the military, to fight for my country. On the other hand, I was still sad I had to leave the eleventh grade to join the armed forces. When I was drafted, I had never been away from my family. I was scared. I was frightened about what could happen to me and the possibility of being separated from my family and never seeing them again. I was not alone like other young recruits who had never been away from home. I holstered my fear and followed the orders of my commanding officers. My own personal reward was the notion that I was among the very few blacks in the marines and I was clearly among those who were blazing a path for the black marines who would follow. That alone allowed me to be caught up in the job and the euphoria of the chance to defend freedom and justice in the world.

Those moments of pride were often deflated. They were punctured by racist remarks or acts aimed at keeping us "in our place". I grew up in difficult times back in Arkansas and I was surrounded by racism then. I had no idea it would be as pervasive in the forces that protect our country. I don't know why I expected the military to be better than society as a whole, but I did, and I was sorely disappointed.

It's strange how some memories of poor treatment are etched in my mind. I often remember the moment and the details. I remember the sights and smells and sounds. If you have ever been the victim of racism, you can relate to this sensory experience. It is not something you tend to forget. You might, however, repress the memory until something causes you to relive the moment.

A Marine general, pompous, proud, and decorated with his recently won medals, began to speak to us, not just in a manner that was depreciating, but downright insulting. His first words were, "The Marines have fought courageously and won many battles in the South Pacific, but I knew we were at war when I returned to the States to find 'you people in our uniforms." He went further to embarrass us when he said, "You people have made no contribution to the great heritage of courage of the United States Marine Corps. However, we expect that in your own limited way, you will contribute to the victory we must win in this terrible war." I reflected on those words for months to come and I recount them as having weighed heavily on my mind each and every day I was in the Marines. The words cut right to my soul and left a mark that shall never be removed. It continues to bother me even to this day and burns like a fire all shut up in my bones. That fire would simmer as a reminder of the work I would have to do to make a difference and to help bring about change. Those words, those damnable words are as much a part of my motivation in the struggle for racial justice and freedom as are the constitutional rights that are mine by reason of American citizenship.

The struggle for freedom and justice initiated in World War II, became just as important, once the war was over. In the war, the fight was for the world. After the war, it was more personal. It was for a people to enjoy that for which we had fought a bloody war. "For my people" though the battles mount; the struggle goes on.

The one area where the Marines did not discriminate was in sending young men to war. It didn't matter the color of your skin. When the nation goes abroad to do battle, all hands, even black hands were needed. Because we were in training during a time of war, the training cycle was accelerated to get men out of basic training and into action as soon as possible. My group spent only three months training at Montford Point. We were there to learn the basics and to prepare to ship out. Blacks continued to be trained for service to the fighting marines. While we were prepared and trained in munitions, we were not sent overseas to point a weapon at anyone. As part of the support crew, I was assigned as a depot marine. The members of my battalion would ensure the white soldiers on the front lines would have all they needed to engage in battle. We kept them supplied with munitions and food. We knew the importance of what we had to do and we did it well. We were a cohesive group who worked as one. Rarely did we receive accolades for a job well done. Instead we were put to work – did our jobs and then given another assignment. Perhaps one day our nation will pay true homage to those men who were like me, among the first to serve the marines. Perhaps we will finally be given our due and a rightful place in the annals of history. For now though, we relish the pride of a job well done – regardless of whether we will ever be recognized for the vital role we played in this theater of war thousands of miles away from home.

Three months after arriving at the base in North Carolina, we received orders to immediately join the conflict. By this time in 1942 the war had moved to the Solomon Islands in the Pacific. The Japanese had landed and occupied several areas in and around the Solomons. They built naval and air bases. The allie's supply and communication lines were threatened in the South Pacific. We were among the warriors sent there to reclaim these areas. It was a major part of World War II. The black marines' unit continued to man the supplies and was attached to the Third Marine Division. Our shield said it all, Fidelity, Honor, Valor. The Fighting Third, as it became known, was a hellish group of men who took the fight to the enemy and through skill, prayer, and sometimes just luck managed to bring about victories in battles known and unknown.

The whole time I was overseas, my mind would drift on occasion back to Little Rock and I would wonder about my brothers. All six of Lula Belle's sons were overseas at the same time.

While I was in Guam, my brother Henry was in Burma and India. Olee was in New Guinea and New Zealand. Sam went from the United States to England, to France and then to Germany. Meanwhile, David was moved from his U.S. base to North Africa, then to Italy and on to Germany. Mama had received letters from her sons tracking their movements. When she realized that both David and Sam were in Germany at the same time, she wrote to David and he in turn hitchhiked to Sam's location. To my recollection, that was the only time during the war any of us made contact with each other.

Mother kept track of us all, receiving letters from each of her sons who did the best they could at keeping her informed of the news from the war front. The whole time we were away Lula Belle was in prayer. There were times when she would stand up in her church and offer her testimony. This woman had six sons fighting in a war that spanned the globe and she was bound and determined to pray us safely home. In her testimony, mother would tell the members of her church that we were at war and she was compelled to have special prayer sessions just for us. She would announce that she would be at the church on a Saturday afternoon and sometimes forty or fifty people would show up. They would gather for an hour or two and each one would stand up and offer prayer for us and for all the other men and women whose lives were in harm's way – a long way from home. I imagined these were emotional heartfelt prayers. Some of the worshippers did not have a relative fighting in the war, but they were praying for "their sons," the sons of the church, the sons of Lula Belle Sutton and the sons of people they didn't even know. The prayers must have worked because as time marched on, Lula Belle and the church members prayed her sons home safely. All six left, all six returned to the awaiting arms of their mother. Olee was the only one who was injured. He was near a bomb attack and his legs were damaged by shrapnel from the bomb. He recovered and eventually returned to Little Rock.

Further proof of the power of prayer was the fact that each of us had stories of how we were near danger and escaped unharmed. On one oppressively hot day, I was standing guard at the supply depot in Guam. The Japanese soldiers had been practically decimated and were forced into the thick jungles of the hills. We didn't know how many of them were there, but we knew they were watching us. Guard duty was a serious thing. You never knew when someone would try to raid the camp and destroy or simply steal our supplies including, food, clothing, artillery, and ammunition.

While standing there, I heard a mighty explosion; the ground rocked and the noise was deafening. It happened in the blink of an eye. Soldiers were running for cover, grabbing their weapons and ready to fire. I took cover and was prepared to take aim. I couldn't see through the smoke and then came falling debris. There was no target, no sign of an enemy. Metal and fire rained down on me like a mighty storm. Not once was I hit, not a single scratch. I knew as soon as the smoke cleared and things settled down that there was a reason that I was not hurt. Here I was thousands of miles away from home…all alone really, in a foreign land and longing for the familiarity of my life that so defines who I am. But right here in this instant….a moment that could have ended so differently I came face-to-face with the stark and sobering reality that at any moment my life could come to an end.

My thoughts on this probably took only a few minutes, but it felt so much longer. It has been said that sometimes tragic events in your life cause you to have an epiphany, a recollection, a realization. That blast and the closeness to death that was brought to my eyes and my ears caused me to know this. I am not alone. I am not in this world going about my business and making it through on my own volition. There is a guiding force, a power and it felt oh so familiar. I knew that there were those who were thinking of me. I knew and felt the presence of the woman who had given me birth and brought me this far on my journey.

The power of prayer is described in so many ways. It is a personal experience and means something different to everybody. I have always known about the power of prayer, but it is yet another thing to feel it. I felt it that day. I am of the firm belief that I was there, tossing these thoughts around in my head because my Mama was praying for me. The powers of her prayers were felt, deep in my soul and when I closed my eyes, I thanked my God for protecting me and for following the orders of that incredible woman and all her friends who fell to their knees and sent up – the power of prayer.

"THE END OF THE WAR"

From The Solomon Islands, I went to Saipan and from Saipan to Guam and from Guam to Iwo Jima. I remember, very vividly, the day when the war ended. It was August 15, 1945. It was a grand day when it ended. Around the world leaders were giving the news to constituents. In Japan people heard about the end of the war in a recorded message from Emperor Hirohito.

Chinese Chairman of the National Military Council, Chiang Kai-shek launched a radio address to proclaim that "Our faith in justice through the black and hopeless days of eight long years of struggle has been rewarded." The word spread from continent to continent – from country to country and rang throughout villages and towns and across backyard fences.

At that time I happened to be on guard duty on Guam. When the guards came with our relief at 2 a.m., they were jovial and making a lot of noise. The first news of what had happened rang in my ears as one of my fellow marines yelled, "Ozell the war is ended!" It was my relief guard coming on duty for the remainder of the night.

"You don't know what you are talking about," I said. When I got back, the guys at the camp were rowdy. They were firing their guns into the air in celebration. The deafening sound rang out for miles and others joined in on the celebration. I never have been one to like that kind of activity. But I was glad. The Marines were taking island after island. I knew we probably did not have long to stay there. At the camps, the guys continued to party throughout the night and into the early morning hours. They sang and talked about their trips home and of loved ones they longed to see once again.

On August 6, 1945, President Truman had made the decision that would trigger the surrender of the Japanese and bring this horrid war to an end. The sad thing is that these actions would result in tremendous loss of life. For the first time, the United States would use the nuclear power it had held in its arsenal. It was called "Little Boy" – and was harnessed inside the belly of a B-29 Super-fortress called the Enola Gay. This massive four engine propeller-driven bomber would fly over the city of Hiroshima and drop its payload. Eighty-thousand people died and more than 65% of the city's buildings were destroyed. Three days later at 11:02 a.m., a second bomb was dropped on the city of Nagasaki. Forty-thousand people were killed. Before the war was over, hundreds of thousands of people would die.

I could only imagine what a fright the bomb instilled in the people of Japan. That prevented us from going to the beaches of Japan because we knew it was going to be a bloody struggle. Because the closer we got, the harder the Japanese fought. We knew that some blood was going to flow on the Japanese shores and some of that was going to be ours, as well as their blood.

I was saddened by the loss of life in Japan, but I was glad when the war was over and the enemy surrendered. I stayed over there 6 months after the war. I went from Iwo Jima back to Guam. The military was releasing soldiers based on a point system. The soldiers with the most points went home first. You got one point for each month of service in the state, two points for each month overseas and 10 points for each child you had. I went in 1944 and the war ended 1945. I had no children and was not married. So, I had 37 points. Others had 70 or 80 points with two, three and four children and more time as an active duty serviceman.

In my upbringing, my mother, my greatest teacher always told me that God will provide and he would protect me no matter how far away from home I might be. Although I was scared, I carried that belief with me thousands of miles away from Arkansas to the shores of a distant land. She was right; God was with me and guided my way through the training in North Carolina. He blessed me with traveling mercies as my Marine company was ferried on the ships and planes into battle, and then through the process that brought the war to an end. He would be with me for many more years and many more battles. The war for me was over, no more supporting troops in foreign lands. I was determined that my military service was over. As a young man, I wanted to join the forces that protected this country. I wanted to be in the number of men who had joined the armed forces and came home with a yarn to spin about the hardships of war, staring at the face of the opposition and then returning home a hero. I was and still am proud of my country, but I knew there was a better way to serve. I was going home, destined to do battle in a different war; a war for equality and justice on terra firma – on land I recognized. It would be a war fought not in the fields of a foreign country, but at home on streets and in alleys and courtrooms and classrooms. It would emanate from the narrow lanes and dusty roads in the countryside to the wide streets and bright lights of major cities. It was to be a distinctly American war where lives were lost and lives were saved and the laws of the land would be put to the test. All this coursed through my mind as I threw a well worn duffle bag onto the metal floor of a massive ship. The waves would lull me into sleep and I would dream of what was to come. The first conflict would arrive soon after I got home.

COMING BACK HOME

After days at sea, the ships finally landed in California bringing troops home from the war. There was much celebrating on board. We all talked about what we wanted to do when we finally got home to loved ones. We talked of food, and friends, and of course, women. There was no grand welcome home for the black marines. We arrived on the west coast not far from San Francisco and everyone had to find a way to get back home the best they could. I got a train ticket and rode the rails for three days, happy to be back in the United States and even more excited about getting back to Little Rock. I crossed this country looking out the windows at the land beyond the rails. There were places I had never before seen and places I would never see again. There was even more time for reflection and contemplation about who I am and who I wanted to be. I never arrived at a definitive answer – but I knew the kinds of things I wanted to do. I wanted to help care for my family. I wanted to ensure their comfort and perhaps start a family of my own. Most importantly, I wanted to put the fervor for change that churned inside me to use. Things had to change in this country for my people. If I could fight a war overseas, I should be regarded as a worthwhile citizen no matter where I went in the United States. I was continually angered at the way people who look like me, who built the country, who cared for its people, and raised its food and its children, were treated. I couldn't solve this dilemma right now for the motion of the train lulled me back into slumber. Rest would give me clear vision and after all I was near home...and soon to be back in the arms of my mother and sisters and brothers.

The train arrived at the depot just before dawn. The people of Little Rock are early risers and this day was no different. People were moving in the city and barely a head turned when I, the black marine, stepped down from the rail car with a duffel bag over his shoulder. I paused for a moment to breathe in the air of the land of my birth. There is nothing like being home. I took an early bus from the station to my house. The bus stop was three blocks from my house. I grabbed my bag and began the short walk. With every one of my steps closer to home, I began to notice every little thing. I looked around in amazement at the houses and the trees and never once thought about the horror of war I left thousands of miles away. The streets were relatively quiet as my little neighborhood was waking up for the day. There were no bursts of gunfire in the distance and no bombs, just the sounds of birds and cars, and the familiar smells of breakfast cooking in kitchens where people were preparing for work and school. I approached the house that I had so longed to see and was even more pleased to capture the vision of a familiar face right there waiting on me. Lula Belle Sutton– standing tall with faint tears beginning to well up in her eyes. Her baby was home. No banners, no band, no large crowd; just Lula Belle and a hot meal. That was all I needed. I ate and I slept in my comfortable bed, anxious to resume the life I started before the interruption of war.

During my active duty time in the Marines, I kept in my mind that this was not to be my life. I knew there was something better for me and it was not the military. I desperately needed to get back on my path to my diploma and to make my way through college. I had the words of many people engrained in my psyche that education was the key to setting things right with our people. Long before me, so many others had proven that fact, Booker T. Washington, George Washington Carver, Langston Hughes and so many more. I had my mind set on my determined path and nothing would deter me from it.

I eventually made it back to Little Rock in the summer of 1946 yearning to finish high school. I was in the eleventh grade when I got drafted and took the oath to protect the United States of America. I was 20 years old and entered high school at night. The Veterans Program allowed me to complete my high schooling at the prestigious and much respected Dunbar High School. I could have gotten a high school equivalency diploma. But I wanted a regular diploma. So from September 1946 to January 1947, I set a course on an accelerated track. I was on a roll. I eventually went to Dunbar Jr. College and finished in three semesters, taking 20 and 21 semester hours and working as a cook at night. I remember going to the dean to get permission to carry 20 to 21 hours.

The dean said, "Ozell, I cannot let you do that."

I told him, "I need to do that. I can do it."

He said, "You cannot carry 20 hours and work from 4 p.m. until midnight."

I said, "I can do it." I told him I could. I told him I would come back with a proposal. I said, "If I don't bring you a B average, you can cut me to 16 hours, but if I bring you a B average, you will let me carry twenty-one?" At first, he denied my petition but then acquiesced and decided to let me give it a try. At the end of the semester I had 5 A's and a B plus. He looked at it and said, "I be damned you did it!"

He said, "I was the principal at your high school and I don't remember your being that much into your studies."

I said, "I was just another high school student who made C's. A 'C' was alright then. But now a 'C' is not alright. I can and shall do much better than that!"

He continued to allow me carry the twenty-one hours. I started out as a math major and physics minor. But I wanted to study law, and an advisor suggested to me I get into social science. I wanted to be a civil rights attorney. I wanted to be the next Thurgood Marshall. I was very active as a youth in the National Association for the Advancement of Colored People, the NAACP, and followed the actions of Marshall. So, I changed my major. I finished in three semesters from Philander Smith College in 1950 with a major in political science and three minors in physics, math and philosophy. I was rolling. I was determined. Success was driving me. I had a sense of my destination. I saw my mission, which stayed my mission. But I was not allowed to pursue it. I tried three times to enter the Little Rock Law School. They would not admit me.

There is something about being denied that pushes you to greater heights. I believe that everything happens for a reason. At the time you endure your struggle it is difficult to see, not only the outcome but the possibilities that rise from denial and oppression. Perhaps God never intended for me to become a lawyer. If that be the case, then certainly his vision for me in this world would become manifest in some way. I realized his plan for me could be bigger than I could ever imagine. All I had to do was to stay focused and remember the words of Langston Hughes' "Freedom Plow." It is a beautiful work that speaks to me and speaks of me:

"When a man starts out with nothing,
When a man starts out with his hands
Empty, but clean,
When a man starts to build a world,
He starts first with himself
And the faith that is in his heart-
The strength there,
The will there to build.

First in the heart is the dream-
Then the mind starts seeking a way."

And then at the end of this lengthy prose we find:

A long time ago,

43

An enslaved people heading toward freedom
Made up a song:
Keep Your Hand On The Plow! Hold On!
The plow plowed a new furrow
Across the field of history.
Into that furrow the freedom seed was dropped.
From that seed a tree grew, is growing, will ever grow.
That tree is for everybody,
For all America, for all the world.
May its branches spread and shelter grow
Until all races and all peoples know its shade.
Keep your hand on the plow! Hold on!

All the time I had been in school I was keenly aware of the struggle happening outside the college campuses where I was matriculating. I had always been involved in the premier organization that fought for civil rights – The NAACP. There also was another organization that had its roots in the north but had refocused its energies on the south after the war. Its name is "CORE," an acronym for The Congress of Racial Equality. CORE was an interracial group less popular than the NAACP, nevertheless, its members were also committed to the struggle. CORE concentrated on the treatment of blacks at the polls, and the fact that in many southern states people of color were being denied their voting rights. The vitality of youth kept these organizations alive and I was right there in the middle of it all. My college days were split between my studies, my job, and my quest to be an important part of the Civil Rights Movement. After the war, black men who had fought for the rights of others were more keenly attuned to the fact that they faced the same battles in their homeland. These men came home hyped up about the struggle that lay before them. They had worn the uniform of these United States, but still could not enjoy the freedoms and privileges guaranteed by the Constitution and the Bill of Rights. On many a night, thousands of miles away from home, in the stillness of the night we would take up this issue in our end-of-the-day discussions. We talked about what we would do when we got home. We deemed this as more than just casual conversation. It was more than just something to do to pass the time while on guard duty or working in the vast warehouses moving supplies. It was the foundation for the rest of our lives. It was our new mission. How could we don the uniform designated for battle, a symbol of strength for the nation and yet – not display that same courage when it comes to the oppression of a people? Most of us had some formal education. We wanted more when we returned. We were resigned to the fact that this would be the foundation for change and that we could not speak for others if we were not educated and dedicated to the cause of education for others. The America that sent us to war could ill afford the battle it would face on its own soil. The bloodshed abroad would pale in comparison to the loss of life at home. We were trained in battle and steeled in the belief that we were due a better treatment when we returned home. We left our homes – farms and hamlets – inner city tenements – rural shacks as inexperienced boys who would return as men – men of purpose – men of conviction, and we shall not be moved. Now please don't interpret this as, 'we were coming home for a physical fight' – to the contrary. We had seen enough violence. We were ready for the intellectual battle coupled with the power of people in numbers who shared the same vision and purpose. These were people who heretofore had not been rallied and who knew there could be change, but lacked the voice. Ours would be a mighty voice that would increase in volume and timbre by our sheer numbers and our determination to stay the course and see the mission to its completion. Right was on our side. God was in our heart and in our spirit and it was time for things to change. It was time.

MEETING JOANNA

I wasn't really looking for a girlfriend. I had a number of friends but nothing to speak of in the way of romance. I had tried my best to stay focused on all the tasks on my plate and not get distracted – even by the fairer sex. Like most things in my life, there have been opportunities that were placed before me that I never expected and never sought. Little did I know that stopping in a café for a bowl of chili would lead to a love and marriage that continues to last for more than sixty years.

The choices of places to eat for black people were few. We either ate at home or knew of the handful of places where we could actually sit and enjoy a meal. Forget the linen tablecloths and fine crystal. That simply was not an option for us, nor was many of us accustomed to this type of finery. For me the goal was always and still remains finding a place to dine where the food was good, the service was friendly and the cost – well coincided with what is in my pocket.

I decided to stop in at one of my favorite eateries, The College Inn. It was at the intersection of 16th and High streets near the Arkansas Baptist College. This was a popular place for college students and high school students as well; it was sort of our hangout. It was there that my future wife would take her lunch. I started going to The College Inn because they had a good 'chili mac' and it was reasonably priced. One day I was there for my lunch when I saw a young man who I knew sitting in a booth with two young ladies. He invited me to join them. The young ladies were Joanna and Evelyn, they were best friends. We ate and had casual conversation. I did not think anything of it. I say that, but at the same time I have to acknowledge that I took more than the casual observance of one of these young ladies...and ladies they were. I took note of Joanna, young, beautiful and obviously smart. I was able to surmise she would be regularly frequenting The College Inn. As my fate would have it, soon thereafter, I would see how this innocent meeting would bloom into something more spectacular. Joanna and I talked again and we became friends, not really courting, but friendly. And then I would go back over there, and it turned into courting. She was in the eleventh grade and I was a freshman in junior college. Six months later, we decided to get married. She was very education-oriented and sang beautifully. She sang in the college choir and had since she was in the ninth grade. We got married on May 9, 1947 at my church, the Mount Zion Baptist Church in Little Rock; Frederick T. Guy was the pastor. We were married in the pastor's study. It was a small wedding with just a few family and friends. The people who attended were Joanna's mother, grandmother, a couple of aunts and two or three of her friends, my mamma, sister, older brother and three people from school. We got married at high noon. As a matter of fact, the pastor performed the wedding while taking a lunch break from a Baptist conference that was taking place nearby in Little Rock.

I lived just three blocks from the church. But I was so dedicated to my schooling that on the day of our wedding, I actually went to classes that morning. I had a class at 8 o'clock and another at 9 o'clock. Afterwards, I went home, got ready and went to the church. I am not sure whether it was the excitement and nerves of getting married or just plain forgetfulness, but when I arrived at the church, I realized I did not have the marriage license. With an embarrassed look on my face, I excused myself from the pastor's study and ran back home to get the license. From the time I left until the time I returned, I had been gone for 15 minutes. Pastor Guy performed a simple ceremony just as he had done many times before. With the vows exchanged, we set out to return to my mother's house where she had prepared dinner for us. It was nothing fancy, a meatloaf, mashed potatoes, green peas, apple cobbler. And that was the after-wedding dinner. That night there was a band festival with six or seven marching bands. We went to the band festival and that was the wedding day.

I knew early-on that I had made the right decision. Joanna and I complimented each other. I was more outgoing and gregarious, and she was more gentile and refined. We were a perfect match. Joanna stayed in school and the next semester she had our first child. Long before Angela Cassandra Sutton was born, Joanna and I had already determined how her life would be. We wanted nothing but success for our children. We wanted them to have a better life, free from the struggles we faced. Every parent wants that, but we were bound and determined to achieve it for our first born and the two who would follow some five years apart. Joanna dropped out of school to have the child, and after Angela was born she went back to school in January and got her high school diploma. Our mothers were always there to help us in our early life as a family. Joanna's mother, Mary Francis Freeman, and Lula Belle would take turns caring for our children. They were a godsend.

Meanwhile, Joanna went to Dunbar Junior College. She took a job as a teacher at the school of the deaf before she graduated. She would teach from morning to noon. She would teach half of the day and go to school the rest of the day. I took care of the children when she was off at school. I combed hair, cooked and dressed them. Ours was a team effort.

We were like many young couples of our time. We married young, had children and continued to better ourselves through education. It may not have been the way we wanted to reach all these goals, but it was our reality. If we wanted to do something, we had to find a way of making it happen. As a result, even though we had jobs and children, I did not stop pursuing my degrees and she did not stop earning hers. We plugged away at it until we both got it. We knew each other's wants and desires and we respected each other's goals. We supported each other, talked to each other, and advised each other. This was the beginning of a fifty-nine-year marriage that is still counting. We may not have always agreed, but we never let our own thoughts on issues keep us apart. We have never separated, and at this stage...only God can keep us apart.

Joanna is my rock, my shield all of these years. This is yet another example of how, when I go into something, I always ask God for the victory and he has given it to me.

The Reporting Job

Of all the jobs I held from working in the fields as the son of a sharecropper, to washing dishes in a restaurant, to working the supply line in the U.S. Marines – never did I imagine the opportunity to serve as a reporter for a major newspaper. This was interesting because the Arkansas Democrat – a white daily newspaper – became interested in hiring a black staff writer. There were two newspapers on the scene at that time – the Arkansas Gazette and the Arkansas Democrat – The Democrat was the afternoon paper. They were in great competition. The Gazette was the more liberal of the two and had the greatest number of Black subscribers. The two papers were locked in fierce battle, competing for subscribers.

Since The Democrat was struggling more for readers, it decided to find innovative ways of bringing more eyes to its ink. One venue to get more people to pick up the paper was the notion of diversifying its staff and adding a black staff writer. However, the editors had no plans to change the paper's conservative philosophy.

Representatives from the Democrat contacted the closest black college, my alma mater, Philander Smith College. They began their search for a young reporter candidate. The college and the paper agreed that whoever was chosen would have to meet three basic requirements. They would need to have a good working knowledge of English sentence structure. They would have to be an excellent speller and possess some writing ability.

It was the spring of 1950 and I was a candidate for graduation in May. While attending Philander Smith, I had gained a reputation of being able to speak and write well. I had great training in those areas, even from my early days in the one- room school house – on through Dunbar and into college. There seemed to be a greater emphasis placed on one being able to speak and write well. I am of the belief that the best students in college are those who can compose a clear and descriptive sentence and those who can put their thoughts together and perform the spoken word. These were qualities which were drilled into the minds of the students at Philander Smith and many other post secondary schools for Black students.

The president of Philander Smith was the first to hear from the Democrat's recruiters. They were fairly frank in their description of who they were looking for and why. The school looked at this as a great opportunity for one of its students despite the fact that the first qualification for the job was race. My alma mater, like other schools, always hoped that students would be chosen for jobs on the basis of their abilities first and foremost. The president was honest and said to the Democrat – "We do not have a school of Journalism so I can't make a recommendation to you for a journalist."

Then they contacted attorney Robert Booker and presented to him the notion of hiring a black staff writer. Booker was a noted Arkansas attorney and was on the faculty at P-S. They told Bob they understood that Philander Smith did not have a school of journalism but perhaps there was a student who excelled and would make a good candidate. Bob suggested they pursue a student who was good in English – and they would teach them how to become a journalist.

Booker had taught me a number of times and was very familiar with my writing skills. He even commented to the recruiter that he remembered me because of a term paper I had written and it stuck in his memory. At the time, I was a pre-law major with every intention of being a lawyer. Professor Booker gave the recruiter my name without hesitation. I can't remember whether I was more excited about the possible opportunity to write for a newspaper or the fact that I had impressed Bob Booker.

I went down to The Democrat at the invitation of the newspaper's executive editor. I had on my suit of clothes – my tie – I was somewhat nervous. But I have always been very confident about myself. – I believe in me even though I was only 21 years old at the time. To this day, I can tell you very little about that interview. You would think that it was an experience that would stick with me. What I do recall is that the interview did not last a very long time. I must have impressed them because I got the job and soon was preparing myself for the first day as a reporter.

The paper was at the corner of 5th and Scott in Little Rock. The Democrat was very discriminatory like many things were in those days. The office of the Democrat was set up so that the City desk was across the front of the room and the reporter's desks were in a line like a classroom.

It was 1950 and discrimination would not be hidden, even in this newsroom. The paper made no special provisions for me save the fact that they went out of their way to show I was different and at the time not worthy of a place among the other reporters. When I arrived, they put me behind the city desk – away from the other reporters. If you have ever been in a newsroom, there was always the city desk where decisions on which stories to cover were made. The editors sat there and other support staff who run the day-to-day newsroom operations. All of the reporters would be lined up in full view of the city desk. This way the editors and others could see who was there, and who was available to send out on a story at a moment's notice. Well in order to see me, they would have to turn around. I had a clear view of my supervisors' backsides.

My small workspace was the equivalent of the back of the bus; the colored only section. I had a desk and a small manual typewriter and a place to throw my coat. I stayed there for 6 months, working alone with limited interaction with my fellow reporters.

When most writers start reporting, they write about subjects they know and understand. So, I covered my community, black news – persons and personalities. I had no assigned beat. Beats were areas of coverage, like police and the courts, the schools, society news or sports. I would cover whatever I could find. It didn't take me long to realize that while I was frustrated with the treatment and the lack of respect from the staff and the management, I had already made one major contribution to my people. I was one of the first black staff writers for a major newspaper in the south. I knew if I could endure the treatment and all that went with it, there would be others to follow. Other Blacks would come behind me and hopefully, life for them would get easier and easier. They would get jobs as reporters and editors. With their measure of success, they would rise through the ranks of news operations across the country. They would be confident in the fact they were hired because of their ability to write, to turn a story, and their prowess at ferreting out exclusives and not because of the color of their skin. I guess there will always be a measure of having a quota of black faces in newsrooms across the country. The important thing is to get them there and to allow them to report on that which they know, whether it be news of the black community or politics, sports, or world events. I will always read the news, hear the radio reports, and watch the broadcasts with a sense of accomplishment each time I see a black face. It is not enough for me to score a victory for myself. It must have a bigger meaning, a greater result, a far-reaching impact. I have the belief that I paved a way for many a black reporter and I would fight for them at every turn.

Sometimes in life little surprises just happen unannounced. There is no rhyme or reason for their timing, they just happen. It could be bad news or good news. Sometimes it is hard to tell the difference between the two. While something may seem good, it could be bad. Or in the words of my Italian friends... there are times when "It is – what it is!"

One day I entered the newsroom and proceeded to the spot where my desk was supposed to be. But it was not there. My workspace was empty, bare. My first thought was that this was the end. My job was over. But much to my surprise, during the night, someone moved my work station from behind the city desk to beside the city desk. I looked at the editor and decided to make a joke out of the situation.

I said, "Where is my desk? Am I fired?"

Shaken a bit by my comment, he responded, "No, your desk is right here."

I said, "Am I an editor?" He said, "Not hardly!" My attempt at humor had fallen flat, but at least I was amused and at least I was no longer looking at the backside of the editor and the people who worked on the city desk. No explanation was given for the move, it just happened. *"It is what it is!"*

Throughout my days of covering the stories of the black community, I would always look for the little victories. I considered it a victory when a story I wrote was untouched or unaltered by an editor. A front page story was an even bigger victory, which I rarely knew. I managed to change one policy at the paper which elevated my people to their rightful place, and it was all because of a three-letter abbreviation.

The Democrat did not use courtesy titles for black women. Black women were never referred to by "Mrs." They were only referred to by their first name. In my upbringing, it was considered rude and disrespectful to not give a woman a proper salutation whether in a verbal greeting or in a written reference. As a result, I refused to write without using the courtesy title.

As soon as I would put the proper title reference in my stories, the editor would come behind me and strike it out before the story went to print. I would read my stories as soon as they went to print and I was frustrated by these obvious changes and omissions. I was protective of my work and eventually had a fight with the paper over this policy. Editors would daily go through my copy and remove the courtesy title. I did not want to give up easily so, I tried another tactic, another strategy. Instead of me writing "Mrs. Jane Doe," I would instead write "Mrs. James Doe," using the husband's first name rather than the wife's first name. Therefore, if an editor made any changes, it would misidentify the person. The paper prided itself for its accuracy no matter how small. This kind of glaring error would not be tolerated, especially from the segment of the population the newspaper most wanted to attract and keep as subscribers. There were a few times when the editor just routinely went through and deleted the 'Mrs.' from the copy. The story was printed and the subjects of the story were misidentified. How embarrassing it must have been for James Jones to read that he had chaired the women's circle tea party. The error was caught well after the paper went to press.

When I used the women's husband's name, they were somewhat dumbfounded. The executive editor called me in and said, "Dr. Ozell Sutton!" He used the title 'Dr.' as an attempt to be flippant, but yet cordial with me.

I said, "Mr. Litskey – you hired me out of Philander Smith College. You know I am not a Dr." Realizing I was not the least bit amused, he proceeded to say, "We don't use courtesy titles as far as black women are concerned."

"Mr. Litskey you are telling me what the paper's policy is? Well, this is my policy. I will not disrespect a black woman. Now you may do that. But I will not do that. I will give a black woman the same courtesy that you give a white woman. Now if I am fired – I am right here and you can fire me if you want to. But I will not write a woman's name without a courtesy title!"

A few months later, the newspaper changed its policy. I was called in to an editor's meeting and they told me, "Dr. Sutton you have won!" "Mr. Litskey I thank you very much. That relieves a lot of problems that I have and I appreciate that you will now use courtesy titles," I said.

There was absolutely no interaction – between the other reporters and me. I was isolated and I said nothing to anyone. I can only imagine what they were thinking of me. Clearly, I arrived in the newsroom in a different fashion than they. Some of them no doubt had worked many years perfecting their craft even before they were hired to work here. Who knows what difficulties they had to overcome to get here. Or maybe they were hired because of a family connection to the owners of the paper or a high-ranking person in the administration. By whatever means they got their jobs, there was no denying that my first qualification for being considered for employment was the color of my skin. The paper needed me or someone who looked like me. There was no hiding my color, but my desire and my abilities were things that had to be proven and this was no easy audience. To me, I was much like *The Invisible Man* in the literal sense. To many of the staffers, I was invisible, not there; nonexistent. I guess to some of them I was an insult. So there I was all alone trying to make a difference through my writing and the people I covered, *my* people.

My situation contributed to my welfare because I really didn't know anything about reporting but I concentrated on writing. As long as no one was disturbing me, I could concentrate on writing. I endured loneliness in the newsroom for five years. There were times when I was not able to experience the kind of banter found in most newsrooms. I could not bounce an idea off a fellow reporter or get another perspective on a story. I was involved in a singular effort. I would conceptualize a story, research it, get the interviews and then write it all by my lonesome.

I was the only one in the newsroom who knew of my own journalistic short-comings. Everyone else at the paper had some kind of education in the field of journalism. Some had graduated with journalism majors from the University of

Arkansas. I had no real journalism experience, and I was not about to share that with my coworkers. But I listened and learned, and I spent a great deal of time trying to perfect my craft. An important part of that process was good reading skills, sometimes great writing and trying to create my own writing style. I never let on with those reporters that I was secretly learning from them. Much of my writing was feature writing – new things happening to blacks. I became a fairly decent feature writer, even with my lack of formal training and experience. Many reporters will tell you that the best learning in this field is earned by doing. There is no substitute for practical experience. My work was never entered into a formal competition and as a result I won no awards. I am not so saddened by not winning awards, I am more concerned that no one thought that the stories I wrote about the black community was award worthy. Some even believed they were not print worthy – simply because of their subject matter. How could anything in the Black community be important enough to publish in a white newspaper?

Everyone who has ever won an award for journalism did so because they first had great material. The writer is usually glorified when the real star is the subject of the story. The writer would be nothing without the intricacies of someone else's story. That is the case with stories that are written about natural disasters, such as floods, famine, earthquakes, hurricanes and tornadoes.

Many writers have won major awards for their coverage of the worst natural disasters, such as Hurricane Katrina. Who could forget the sight of all those people, all those homes, all that water? It is hard to imagine the death and the devastation of this mammoth storm and the toll it took on cities, large and small throughout the southeast. Even harder to fathom is the response of our leadership. Never before has there been a massive disaster when our own government did not act properly. I tear up with a seething anger when I think of the human suffering in a land that has so many resources. Just think, though, as much as we criticize the media – much of which is admittedly deserved, were it not for their reporting, we may have never known the true degree of deception, deceit, and damage left in the aftermath of Katrina. On a personal note, I also recalled the times when I as a reporter was called upon to cover a tragedy.

As a reporter, I had to be ready to go anywhere and cover anything at a moment's notice. I had to be prepared and versatile. One moment I might be sitting at my desk reading a paper or doing some research or writing my next story when all of a sudden I was shipped out to cover a major breaking event. Sometimes events happen overnight and a reporter can be called out of a sound sleep to cover a story, or it would be the first thing to greet the reporter when he or she walked into the newsroom the next morning.

I faced such a situation on an early morning in Arkansas. There had been a series of overnight tornadoes across the state. Arkansas was ripe with conditions and terrain for these types of storms. Intense summer heat mixed with a rapidly moving storm and the flat terrain made this southern state the back door to tornado alley.

When I arrived at the paper that morning, the editor was calling all of the staff together and sending us out to cover the story. In an unusual move, I was assigned to work with another reporter by the name of Robert McCord. I would normally work alone on a story, so this was a rarity. Our mission was to drive to a small town miles away.

Robert and I became friends on that trip. Although we worked in the same newsroom, there was little opportunity for us to converse and to get to know each other. The newsroom was a place to come, do the job and to go home. I had very little joy working there because the conditions were not ideal for me. I was there as "the black" reporter. Over the years, the hostility of my presence lessened, but I still knew my place. I appeared to be a hard worker just like them. I had proficiency far beyond my training and I treated people with a respect and cordiality that rarely were reciprocated. I guess in their minds that made me alright. As I recall those days, I realize it is easier to gain respect by being professional and competent than trying to gain acceptance through congeniality alone. My lesson learned is that patience is a virtue and that respect is truly earned. During our drive to the scene of the storms, we shared stories of our experiences as reporters and how each of us was raised.

We finally arrived on the scene during the early morning hours and began reporting right away, interviewing people who witnessed the storm and taking pictures of what was left behind.

By ten o'clock in the morning, we realized we had done all this work and had not gotten a single bite to eat. The search was on to find a place that would serve us. I tried to warn McCord that this would be nearly impossible because most places there would not serve a black man.

We went to many restaurants and at each, the servers would take a look at Bob and then look at me and we were denied service. This clearly was the first time that McCord had ever witnessed this. He was very surprised and even tried to force the issue at one diner. He was told he could stay, but I would not be allowed to eat in their establishment no matter who I worked for. At one place they wouldn't even let me come in the door. I told my new friend after several attempts the only way we would get a meal was if he went inside and bought the food and we could eat in the car. At this point my hunger was greater than my pride, plus we are on deadline and needed to complete our task. There is no editor around who would want to jeopardize a story simply because the reporter was hungry. So Robert followed my advice, ordered some food for us, paid for it and took it outside. There in the car – in silence we ate and I knew that this incident affected my colleague. He began to see the world through my eyes and through my experiences. He was sympathetic and darn near apologetic. But all of that meant nothing to the people inside the restaurant. They had their rules and they stuck with them at all cost. For just a moment or two there I thought about all the other people who looked like me who didn't work for a newspaper , who didn't have a white friend to run interference for them in that type of situation. I can assure you that their circumstance could and would have been much worse. The meal was completed. Our bellies were satisfied for the moment. It was time to get back to work.

Within a couple of hours, we returned to the newsroom and had to work on the story. I had taken most of the photographs and Bob wrote the story. I offered suggestions and gave him some of the information I had gathered. The editor came back to my desk and said, "Ozell, I got Bob's story but I didn't get yours. Didn't I send you both to cover the story?" I went to my desk and I began writing. I knew what had been covered in Bob's version, so I took other information he left out and crafted my own.

Mr. Tilden was so impressed with what I had written that my work, for the first time, became the lead story. I can't begin to tell you the number of times I looked down at that paper and admired my by-line. I had seen my name in print many times, but never before above the fold on the front page.

This was truly a turning point for me and my career. More importantly it was the signature event that caused the people in the newsroom to think differently of me. I too thought differently of me. In the eyes of my fellow reporters, I suddenly had value and was more than just someone who could write stories about black people. I was now on a different playing field. I would not be regarded as a star reporter in their eyes, after all – they went to the school of Journalism at the University of Arkansas and I was just a black kid from Philander Smith. But none of that mattered right then, because the by-line at the top of the page read, Ozell Sutton, Staff Writer. The amazing thing about print is that when the ink dries, it is there forever. It was my little mark of immortality. I may move on, but my story will last forever. I can remember standing proudly in the newsroom during the next staff meeting. Mr. Tilden was reviewing our coverage of the tornadoes. He took a moment and held up the paper and gave me a few words of praise. Tilden said to the reporters assembled, "You all did a good job on your stories, but they lacked color. Ozell was both informative and descriptive."

I experienced a small example of my new status the next day in the newsroom. We would often order food out from the Walgreen's food counter at Fifth and Main Streets located just a couple of blocks from the paper. I had often volunteered to pick up the lunch for myself and others. The day after the staff meeting, during lunch time, other reporters offered to pick up lunch for me. I sat down at my desk and placed my order.

I realized all the time I was working at the paper I was carrying the torch for those who would follow. I knew the impact of what I was doing at the time. I was always respected in the black community. I was often praised at black conventions like the NAACP. I would receive acknowledgements from the black churches. I would be refreshed, renewed and retooled to go back into the sometimes hostile newsroom environment.

There were other black people working in the paper, such as handlers and janitors. I may have been discriminated against in the paper, but Blacks had a great appreciation for me. But if they only knew what was being said inside that building. They probably knew how white reporters felt about them, but they never heard it. But I did.

The newspaper staff meetings were often filled with tension, including degrading comments. There was a general staff meeting every Monday morning when the editor would review the past week's performance and projected the week before us. The review was always in comparison to the Arkansas Gazette, the morning version of the Democrat. There was furious competition between the two papers. They were owned by two different companies and each strived to be number one in the state.

During one of our staff meetings, the editor was quite irate. His beef with the staff was over what he termed "the lack of follow-up on stories after they had appeared in the paper for the first time." He specifically mentioned an occasion when two black men were nearly killed in a cave-in downtown where they were digging to cap a water line that had burst underground.

"We were the first to carry the story," he said, "but the next day there was not a follow up story telling the public about the conditions of the two men who were rescued. The public wanted to know if the two Negroes were living or dead," he said. "This is worth another story!" A white reporter standing near me retorted, "Dead is the only way a 'nigger' is worth something!"

There was an immediate hush all over the room. Everyone was perfectly still while those stinging and hurtful words sank in. The silence probably lasted just a few seconds, but it seemed like an eternity. Racial insults were not uncommon in this newsroom coming from reporters who are supposed to be champions of the poor and a voice for the voiceless. But here stood this white man with words of hate dripping from his face and a smirk on his lips as if he had somehow delivered the punch line of a hysterical joke. I was not laughing. I looked at him; straight into his eyes with a piercing look of contempt and disgust. I didn't say a mumbling word and never removed my stare from his face. Sensing my tension and ire for this man, the editor hurriedly dismissed the staff meeting and told everyone to go back to work. That was it. There was no reprimand; there was no call to the office, just a quick dismissal; an avoidance of a problem that would likely be repeated over and over again.

In stark contrast there were those on the staff who had feelings for me and were sensitive to my plight. One by one, these people of goodwill stopped by my desk and offered their apologies for what had happened. Throughout the civil rights movement there were people like this. They were sympathizers who knew the right thing to do. Sometimes they would follow-up on their beliefs and other times their goodwill would not be visible in deeds and work. Many times they feared for their own safety and status in life. They were afraid of what would happen or be said to them if they took a stand and spoke out. I applauded the courage of those who stopped by to offer their help to me that day. I knew the risk they took. It was a scene I would relive on many occasions in the years to come. I knew in a moment, that a part of me wanted to throttle that reporter that day, but somehow my remaining silent sent a louder message than had I resorted to violence. My standing still, holding my ground and keeping silent caused others to marvel at my composure and my self control. This was the infancy of my work for civil rights and equal opportunity. These were the test waters that would challenge my nerve and my resolve to stay strong for myself, for my family, and for my people.

There were people at the newspaper who affected my life, both positively and negatively. The treatment by the paper and the relatively low pay caused me to decide to leave the paper after working there for seven years.

I was seated in the newsroom next to two reporters who experienced significant fame in the field of journalism in Arkansas. On one side of me, the columnist Henry Karr Shannon sat and on the other side was editorial writer Sam Allen. Neither of these two men followed the traditional route one normally follows on the way to the top in a newsroom.

Karr Shannon had studied pharmacy and worked as a pharmacist at a local drug store. He eventually left because of allergies to pharmaceutical chemicals. He left that field and became a teacher and then a principal and eventually was the superintendent of the Izard County schools, all this by the age of 24. Karr later became an attorney and even wrote a couple of books. Karr's views were, shall we say, very conservative. While he boasted he was anti-big government, he rarely sided with politicians. However, he aligned himself on one issue with Governor Orval E. Faubus. Shannon wrote a number of columns against integration. He simply did not see the need for the races to mix together in the classroom. On occasion his columns would bring opposition from people of many races.

Both Shannon and Allen were, like many others in the newsroom conservative, yet cordial and clearly just tolerant of my existence. I don't recall them ever being overtly rude to me, but neither did they strike up a conversation or ask my opinion on the news of the day. To them, I was just there, an object placed between them with little or no value. They had their jobs and I had mine and never did the two meet.

There were times when the story I was covering often would come close to becoming the lead. Many people in town were not used to seeing a black reporter, not to mention one who worked for the conservative Arkansas Democrat. I often covered stories of great controversy. I wasn't always assigned by the editors to cover them, I just did. I was of the belief that if I am to be of service to my people as a reporter, then I would have to cover stories of our community no matter how controversial. Among them was a story of two young black men in rural Arkansas who were on trial for allegedly raping a white woman. Nothing enraged white people more than the mere mention of a black man ever so much as touching or even looking at a white woman. Women were so revered in the white community, so protected, and definitely off-limits to black people. Women represented the purity of the race and the vessels that would bring forth more pure white children. Thus, they had to be protected at all cost.

Add to the mix, the specter of the Ku Klux Klan, who was calling for the lynching of the men without a trial and not so much as a hearing. The racial tension was already high, well before this incident, but now it was immeasurable. The local law enforcement was ready for this powder keg to blow leading up to the trial. The streets were sometimes red with the blood of black people after KKK types roamed the streets randomly grabbing black men and beating them; sometimes to their death. The attacks got little attention from the police because many of the police were Klan sympathizers, if not full members themselves. This kind of vigilante justice was not uncommon in that time and it has been well documented over the years. Good, honest, hardworking, law abiding citizens were sometimes attacked simply because they were on the streets and had committed the audacious and heinous "crime" of merely being black. Staying in their homes was no guarantee of safety either. There had been times when homes were fire-bombed while people inside slept or shots fired in a primitive drive-by shooting. These mobs were no respecters of age or sex. To them the only thing that mattered was the color of their skin.

A tense atmosphere surrounded this case that soon would go before the court. The accused men were represented by the well-known civil rights attorney Wiley Branton. Attorney Branton was born in Pine Bluff. He attended local schools and matriculated at the Arkansas A.M. & N College, which later became the University of Arkansas at Pine Bluff. He received his Bachelor of Science degree from the college and went on to receive a law degree from the University of Arkansas at Fayetteville. This handsome very light-skinned young man was the fourth black student to enroll at the institution and the third black student to graduate. Over the years Branton made a name for himself by taking on and representing people of color in sometimes racially charged cases. It was not uncommon for him to take on cases in small towns where he surely would become a target of hatred and the same racism that brought his clients to trial. Branton was also no stranger to being the target of the law. This learned man fought in World War II, came home, got educated and went to work to help his people. He took the time to teach poor and sometimes uneducated blacks how to mark an election ballot. He was once arrested and charged with "teaching the mechanics of voting". It was this incident that surely propelled him into the spotlight and gave him purpose in receiving a law degree.

The day had finally come. The two black men were set to go on trial. Word spread quickly that Wiley Branton would be representing the defendants. A mob gathered at the courthouse due to the publicity of the case. They were there for the sole purpose of finding Wiley Branton and beating him. They had every intention of insuring these men would be found guilty, either through the laws of the state of Arkansas or the guarantee of street justice. There was also word they planned to grab the two men on trial and hang them even before the trial began.

On the first day of the trial, I decided to cover the proceedings. Most of the people in the mob had no idea what Wiley looked like. There had been very few published pictures of him. Wiley was very light-skinned and walked right into the courthouse unnoticed by the mob. I, on the other hand, was right there standing on the front steps. I, with my very black features, proceeded to walk up the front steps. The mob moved in, figuring I was Wiley Branton. Their voices grew louder. I was surrounded right there in broad daylight on the steps of the hall of justice. I would like to be able to say I was brave and unafraid of the moment, but that simply would not be true. I have seen what a mob can do to a human being. I know of the pain they can inflict, the beating, and the slow death. Yes, I was afraid, but I tried to keep moving. That's when it happened. They pushed me down, and I knew the real torture was about to begin. My mind raced – looking around, glimpsing faces, fists and the deafening sound of human rage. I wondered if the taunts and slurs would be the last sounds my ears would ever hear in this life. I wondered if my life would come to an end on the courthouse steps. I had so much I wanted to do; so much I wanted to change. I could see another man pushing his way into the crowd and yelling for the people to stop, to leave me alone.

"Ozell, what are you doing here?" the voice cried. I made eye contact with him and recognized him as a reporter from the rival Arkansas Gazette. "This is not Wiley Branton! He is Ozell Sutton, a reporter just like me! Branton walked passed you some time ago. He is already inside the courthouse!"

It was this white reporter who saved my life. He came to my aid despite the possibility of being harmed himself. I cannot remember his name, but I shall never forget his face and his deed will remain with me as long as I have breath. This man did what other people would not. There were no blacks there to help me. Most of them knew of the danger this trial would bring and they stayed away. The only black people there were the relatives of the two men on trial and they had been escorted into the court by armed officers.

I never returned to cover that case. I was a young man and I believe I was so shaken that my resolve was shattered, at least for that moment. In the years to come, I would look back and wonder what happened to those men. I am sure with Wiley Branton on their side justice prevailed.

There is so much that people can do to right a wrong. Sometimes it does not take an act of heroism like the reporter. It only takes some caring and a voice to speak out and call injustice by its name. We never know what we can do until we try. This would not be the only time that a white man saved my life. It would happen again. A hand would reach down and pluck me from danger – much like the finger of God – as he reaches down each day and touches me with a finger of love as I slumber and I sleep and allows me to see a new day.

LEAVING THE DEMOCRAT

After seven years at the paper, I came to the realization I could no longer stay there. I have always had the need to progress, to grow both mentally and financially. The job had become stagnant for me, and there was no hope of my advancing through the ranks. I had to face the hard reality of that fact. I fulfilled a need at the paper and it benefited from my having been there. Prior to my arrival there were few black readers of the paper and even more sadly there were no stories to speak of from the black perspective. I provided an insight into the community in which I lived in a way that no other non-black reporter could. I wrote not just about events and people. I wrote about my people and my life. The subjects I profiled, I knew personally. I knew of their upbringing, I knew where they lived. I knew their spouses, their children, their ministers, their cousins, their neighbors. I knew their struggle and I knew their triumphs in spite of difficulty. I told the stories of my people and by doing so, I gave life and breadth to a people who were rarely given a second look and nary a notion of what they had experienced on a daily basis. That is the joy of journalism, giving people, persons, and things a new perspective by detailing an untold story. I loved the challenge of writing and the reward of knowing I had done a good job. I knew there was more for me. I knew I had to get back to the real work of helping people and devoting more time and resources to the struggle for civil rights. That was an avocation I simply could not pursue as a reporter and definitely not while I was working at The Democrat.

I had another consideration. I needed more money, which the paper was not going to provide. Even some of the white reporters complained about the relatively low pay. I had performed the same job for seven years and still barely made ends meet. Sometimes I would get an occasional raise of five or ten dollars a week. We had families and needed to provide for them. Joanna had been understanding during those lean years and now was the time to make a move to improve all of our lives. Our two children were still very young at the time and a part of me wanted to stay in journalism. I tried to go to Chicago and seek a job with Johnson Publication's Ebony and Jet. I soon was turned down by then managing editor Lerone Bennett. I went to the Chicago Defender, but was rejected there as well. Henceforth, I decided to stay in Arkansas and to look for work wherever I could find it. I wanted something where my talents could be used and a job where I could be of greater service to people. I did not find the job I wanted, but one that paid more than I had previously made. It was a job of service; not to a large group of people – but rather for one of the wealthiest men in the country, a man by the name of Winthrop Rockefeller.

I had been looking for work for a while when it occurred to me there was a man who had done great things in Arkansas and perhaps he could be of help to me. I went to the offices of Mr. Winthrop Rockefeller. I was looking for some type of administrative job, but none was available. The executive secretary to Mr. Rockefeller explained what I wanted simply did not exist, but there was one job she thought I could perform well; that of butler to the Rockefeller family. She was so insistent that she put me in her own car and drove me the 65 miles to WinRock, the name of Rockefeller's farm on Petit Jean Mountain. It was the official residence and retreat for W. R.

Winthrop Rockefeller was born into wealth. His family truly had a household name. He is the fourth son of John D. Rockefeller, Jr. John D. is best known as the founder of Standard Oil Company, an industry giant that made billions of dollars. The family is also well known for it's commitment to people and became among the country's best known philanthropists. John D. Rockefeller had an interesting philosophy when it came to helping people. He even wrote it down in a statement that became a cornerstone for his children, including Winthrop.

I Believe
By John D. Rockefeller, Jr.

I believe in the supreme worth of the individual and in his right to life, liberty, and the pursuit of happiness.

I believe that every right implies a responsibility;
every opportunity, an obligation; every possession, a duty.

I believe that the law was made for man and not man for the law; that government is the servant of the people and not their master.

I believe in the dignity of labor, whether with head or hand; that the world owes no man a living but that it owes every man an opportunity to make a living.

I believe that thrift is essential to well ordered living and that economy is a prime requisite of a sound financial structure, whether in government, business or personal affairs.

I believe that truth and justice are fundamental to an enduring social order.

I believe in the sacredness of a promise, that a man's word should be as good as his bond; that character – not wealth or power or position – is of supreme worth.

I believe that the rendering of useful service is the common duty of mankind and that only in the purifying fire of sacrifice is the dross of selfishness consumed and the greatness of the human soul set free.

I believe in an all-wise and all-loving God, named by whatever name, and that the individual's highest fulfillment, greatest happiness, and widest usefulness are to be found in living in harmony with His will.

I believe that love is the greatest thing in the world; that it alone can overcome hate; that right can and will triumph over might.

Winthrop Rockefeller was a giant of a man in both his stature and his belief. He broke many molds and surprised the wealthy elite when he served in the armed forces. Win joined the Army and was right there in the thick of things on the front lines of World War II. We never met during the war but, ironically, we were among the thousands of soldiers who were sent to the South Pacific. In 1945, he survived a Japanese kamikaze bombing of his troop transport ship just before returning home. For many years Win ran the family business in New York. He soon grew tired of the "New York Crowd" and in 1953 at the invitation of an army buddy, moved to Petit Jean Mountain and built WinRock Farms. The ranch became one of the premier producers of Santa Gertudis cattle. Soon after moving there, Win became a well-known corporate citizen and ran the Arkansas Development Commission. He was credited with attracting more than 600 industrial plants and 90,000 jobs to the state. I wanted to work with Winthrop Rockefeller for this very reason. I felt he could help me to grow and develop and further the cause of civil rights.

When we arrived at the farm, I was ushered into the office of Winthrop Rockefeller. After a brief conversation about my background and my youth, I was offered the job. Surely this happened based on the recommendation of the executive secretary.

As I look back on it today, I often wondered what I said or did to make them want to hire me. After all, Arkansas is Arkansas, and I was a poor black man in need of a job. I did have a number of skills that separated me from the average black man of that day. I was educated, I had writing skills, I spoke well, and I was a great study of people and people's needs. I was so confident that I challenged Winthrop Rockefeller to increase his salary offer. I hadn't even gotten the job and was already asking for a raise. I was clear on my needs and had calculated my own expenses to the penny. I had to. According to my calculations, I needed $25 more a week than he was offering. We talked about it for quite a while. I remember it because I even said, "Surely a man of your means can afford to pay $25 more a week."

Surprised at my candor he quickly retorted, "Of course, I can afford it! But if you look at the fact that I have hundreds of employees and if I paid everyone $25 more a week, well then we'd be talking about a significant amount of money."

There was a slight pause and a shift in his eyes, a glance out the window and then back at me. He ended "But you will get your $25." Satisfied with myself and his response, I prepared for the ride back to town to tell Joanna that I had a new job.

For 20 years, Win Rockefeller called 927 acres home. This billionaire sought to make a difference in what was once the poorest state in the union. With his considerable influence, Win brought national leaders to this rural mountainside to talk about ways to improve Arkansas. A captain of industry, he influenced other corporations to locate here. He also tried to harmonize the races, train farmers, and address a wide range of environmental issues.

My position at WinRock was that of a butler. I was never trained to hold that title, but throughout my life I have done numerous jobs that prepared me for this moment. I had cooked, washed dishes and cleaning was something I did well. Lula Belle had often said the greatest service is service to human beings. It was with that thought that I ventured into this new position. WinRock was a spectacular place.

I worked very hard at WinRock, that's the only way I knew how to work. A butler was not my goal in life, but for now it was my life. This is where I am and I will make the most of it and perform the job with pride and dignity. I sometimes look back and realize that this was part of God's plan for me. This is where I was supposed to be at that moment and stage of development in my life. I guess one of the hardest things for people to do is to be happy where they are. Sometimes we take our blessings for granted and always look for what's next in our lives and not where we are. For the day and time this was a good job with good benefits. I was here not only to be of service, but to learn. I was surprised at what I learned by being in the company of such an influential person. I realized that by being silent and paying attention, I could and did learn. After all, Win Rockefeller was where I wanted to be and most assuredly I could learn a fraction of what he knew.

There was much said about Winthrop Rockefeller. His actions were well-published in the newspapers and definitely were the topic of discussion all around Arkansas. Word spread quickly when Winthrop Rockefeller came to town. For many what happened on Petit Jean Mountain was a mystery, but everyone soon learned this was a man who wanted to affect change and he did it with great style and grace.

The Rockefeller family treated me with great respect. I admired them. They looked at people as people. And they demanded that of their staff as well.

There were some grand gatherings at WinRock. Some of them were purely social, others were to further the cause of development in rural Arkansas. Whatever the case when it came to events, Ozell Sutton was in charge. I was responsible for every aspect of major events. In my charge were some 25 staff people plus anyone else who was brought in as part of the catering staff. We would serve as many as 300 people at a time and each event was flawless. Southern hospitality dictates that guests are made to feel special and their every need be met. Service was always with a smile and reflective of the atmosphere the Rockefellers had initiated in their time on this grand estate.

The planning for events would many times begin with a meeting between Mrs. Rockefeller and me over a meal. I recall once when we were beginning this process, Mrs. R, as I referred to her, suggested we have lunch outside next to the pool and under a large tree.

"I just love dining outside under the trees, don't you Ozell?" she said in a sophisticated tone not heard much in these parts.

Without hesitation I interjected with the kind of abrupt Ozell-like response that often speaks and later explains. "No ma'am, I don't!"

"Well why not Ozell? It's such a lovely day"

She sat down on a chair near the door leading outside and I told her my story. She listened with genuine interest and intrigue.

"Mrs. Rockefeller, I was raised as a sharecropper with my family. I would often work on various farms and I did everything from chopping cotton, to planting the soil, to plowing the fields. As you know when we plowed the fields, we would have to start early in the morning and try to beat the heat of the day. We took very few breaks – mostly just a moment or two to get a drink of water and then right back into the field. I would bring a pail with my lunch in it and stash it somewhere out of the sun until time to eat. In those days there was no such thing as eating inside, there was no inside except for the main house or a barn. I could not have gone inside to catch a break from the sun and the oppressive heat. I was allowed to bring an old mule up to the house where there was water and he could rest. But I was told the only place to eat my lunch was a great distance from the house and under a tree. The farm animals were closer to the house than I was allowed. I sat under those trees so much and I thought and I pondered my life and I made a decision one day. I vowed when I was on my own, and became an adult, I would never eat outside again under a tree. For me it brings back too many bad memories of those days gone by. It was a time when black people were treated worse than the farm animals and we were expected to take it, to accept it and to like it. Well, I didn't like it one little bit. So, Mrs. Rockefeller, I mean you no harm, but if you please, I will have my lunch inside the house and we can talk about the party anywhere you like, as long it is not outside under a tree."

Astonished at this story, Mrs. Rockefeller acquiesced and never again did we meet outside. The next party was a big one. I was responsible for 30 waiters, 10 bartenders and the hundreds of guests. We had a huge tent outside to accommodate this event and like many in the past and many to come, it was a grand affair. I took a moment and looked at the activity, the white-gloved service, the candles and the splendor of it all. I pondered the thought that one day, people will provide this kind of service for me. I will always be of service to people, but there will be waiters, butlers and bartenders in my future. And I will enjoy and be honored by their courtesy.

I must have done a good job for the Rockefellers, because I worked for Winthrop on three different occasions. During my second stint at WinRock, I was asked by the Rockefellers to move my family to the plantation. It was quite a drive from Little Rock to Petit Jean Mountain, some 50 miles. This would be much more convenient and I could spend more time with my young family. This gesture of housing was also another example of the giving spirit of the Rockefellers. If the Rockefellers had it, we had it. The meals in the main house were the same as the meals in my house. I was able to care for my family there in a way I could not have had they lived in town. This was a good arrangement for me.

Shortly after my family moved to WinRock, Joanna was given a contract to teach shortly after we moved to WinRock to teach in the Morrilton School

System. Mr. Rockefeller was trying to create a model school district with large supplementary grants. It was during the troublesome time.

At that time school desegregation was the biggest racial issue in Arkansas. Governor Orval Faubus poisoned the racial climate in the state and the state legislature passed laws stating that no state employee could belong to the National Association for the Advancement of Colored People, the NAACP. The Attorney General, who also wanted to be governor, went on to crusade against desegregation.

Integration of the schools had become the law of the land. All across the country, schools were becoming racially mixed. The process was slow and in some cases dangerous. White families were pulling their children out of schools that were to be integrated. Riots broke out across the south as little children tried to achieve the most basic of rights. Homes were burned, people were threatened, and champions of integration were beaten and intimidated. It was a violent and scary time. At every legal turn, politicians against integration created state laws to supersede federal laws. Even the President of the United States was at a loss for a quick solution to this problem.

It was in this atmosphere the Orval Faubus made some of his most infamous comments and people like Winthrop Rockefeller was working to keep the calm and bring about peaceful change. Winthrop invited me to have lunch one day and made it clear he wanted to discuss my wife's employment with the school system. We sat in a private dining room with only the staff there to serve us. My host was cordial and accommodating as always, but it was clear to me by his demeanor there would soon be a serious discussion. I knew that no matter what his plan, he would be fair. He didn't have to be, but it was in his nature to look at all sides of an issue before making a decision on anything.

In an effort to fulfill his responsibility to us, and at the same time not lose political followers in this frantic southern state, he offered to give Joanna a fellowship to do further study at any university she chose. It was no secret that Win Rockefeller wanted to be governor of Arkansas. In making this offer he sought not to alienate large segments of the constituency. He asked forthrightly whether Joanna was a member of the NAACP. I confirmed that she was. He reminded me of the law passed by Orval Faubus making it illegal for any state employee to belong to the NAACP. He again made the offer of a grant for Joanna's continued education.

I pondered this for a moment taking into account what this man was up against and of course my loyalty to the NAACP and the cause of human rights and justice. We both were after the same thing, but certainly from different perspectives. His was a future leader who would eventually be responsible to every citizen in the state, of all races, and of all interests. I, on the other hand, was responsible to a more targeted population that began right inside my little house and extended to hundreds of thousands of other people who looked just like me. This man was my employer and he would have been full within his rights to fire me for what I was about to say. However, I also knew that his thinking was more global and that he had a loyalty to those who were loyal to him.

I chose my words carefully and responded that my wife had signed a contract to teach as a state employee in the fall. She had every intention of honoring her contract and would be in the classroom. I could not accept his offer if it meant turning my back on my people. We had come too far to allow our comfort to dictate our stance on civil rights. I informed him that we were prepared to fight this action with the state and its racist law. Winthrop Rockefeller took a pause and then without hesitation said, "All right, we will fight, if necessary and I will finance the fight!"

At that very moment Winthrop Rockefeller dove into the pool with all the rest of us working to make things better for all people in Arkansas. If this billionaire and his butler had no mutual respect for each other, the meeting could have had a very different outcome. Instead, the situation stood as an example of what people are capable of if they demonstrate their commitment and willingness to take risks and to step into harm's way for the greater good.

CENTRAL HIGH SCHOOL CRISIS

All the time I worked for the Rockefellers, I maintained my membership in the NAACP. I was actually more than just a member, I was an active participant. The NAACP was the premier organization working for civil rights at the time.

This organization had come a long way by the time I became a member. Many people would be surprised to know the first meeting to formulate this organization was actually held in Canada. Thirty-two prominent and out-spoken African Americans decided in 1905 the time had come to discuss the challenges facing colored people in the United States, including segregated hotels. So noted scholar W.E.B. DuBois convened the meeting in a hotel on the Canadian side of Niagara Falls. That was the beginning of what became "The Niagara Movement". Three white people became early members and shared the concerns of DuBois and his followers. After three years of meeting in various places, the Niagara Movement was finally formalized on the 100th birthday of Abraham Lincoln; February 12, 1909. In 1910, the name National Association for the Advancement of Colored People was adopted.

The early years of the NAACP were spent using the courts to overturn Jim Crow laws that legalized racial discrimination. Membership grew by leaps and bounds as local chapters sprang up all over the country. The nation was caught in the grips of anger and hate perpetrated by those who wanted to keep things the way they were. Lynchings were rampant in the south in the early 1900's and the NAACP was there to force the courts to help bring those who murdered to justice. Next came the efforts to enforce voting rights laws. Federal laws were ignored in some states and blacks were prevented from registering. Other states created "grandfather laws" that basically stated if your grandfather was not allowed to vote, neither were you. The NAACP used the laws of the land to protect the people and their rights. Those opposed to equal rights were equally as vigilant to create loopholes and counter laws.

Years before the integration of schools in Little Rock, there has been a number of integration challenges and small victories for equality. In September of 1949, the school of law at the University of Arkansas was integrated and in 1951, the Little Rock Public Library approved integrating its facilities.

The greatest test for the NAACP would be the desegregation of schools. Little Rock would become the center of attention on this issue as we sought to integrate Central High School. There was one woman who initiated this long and sometimes dangerous prospect. She was one incredible woman by the name of Daisy Bates.

Daisy was an unusually strong woman considering what she endured in her early years. Daisy lost her mother when she was just a young girl. Three white men tried to rape her mother. She fought them and in the process was killed. Her father was obviously distraught and eventually left the family never to return. Daisy was raised by family friends. This beautiful young woman drew the attention of many young men, including one by the name of L.C. Bates whom she married in 1942. Little Rock was their home. They established the Arkansas State Press, a local newspaper that played a pivotal role in the lives of people in the area. The paper was a strong voice in the fight for civil rights. L.C. and Daisy would publish violations of the Supreme Court's desegregation rulings much to the ire of the mainstream press and the local governments who violated the laws.

Daisy Bates would eventually become involved with the NAACP and rose to be its local president. Daisy had a fire in her that would not be quenched until black people were treated fairly in accordance with the laws. So it came as no surprise that she would lead the most controversial movement to date in the history of Little Rock. She would, with the help of legions of concerned citizens, facilitate the integration of Central High School.

From my years shortly after returning from World War II, I was determined to be of service in some way to people. I knew of the struggles that existed for my people. I was aware of the changes that people were trying to make in the quest to make life better for people of color. What I didn't know was exactly how I would fit in, but I knew there was a place for me and that I had energy, will, and talent to lend to the struggle.

I was changed because I saw and experienced racism with my own eyes. I realized very quickly that I was a part of a group of people whose standing in the community has been discounted. I was being hated simply because I possessed more melanin in my skin or I came from another country or was in some way different from the people who wanted to harm me. Oppression is a horrible thing. The notion that one human being is somehow better, or greater, or more valuable than another is senseless and degrading. Some even used the bible as a basis for carrying out their beliefs. I could not fathom a higher power suggesting such a thought.

I first entered the NAACP as a young man and student at Dunbar Junior College. Soon after that I moved to Philander Smith and established the first ever college chapter of the NAACP in Arkansas. Recruiting members was no problem. The students at Philander Smith all had come from similar backgrounds. We all knew of the struggle for equal treatment in all aspects of our lives. Many of us had been rejected from other colleges; others followed in family traditions and went to Philander Smith as a fulfillment of a family legacy. For whatever reason, these young minds were brought to the institution. We were united in our beliefs and our desire to be the generation of change. We had the hope of being remembered in history as the people who righted the wrongs of our day.

We all quickly began working with the youth council. Young people were encouraged through the organization to enhance self through various programs. The NAACP is widely known as an organization that trains the next group of leaders. It is part of our heritage to raise, teach and preserve our heritage. The NAACP was doing much more by involving teenagers in the structure of the organization and giving them leadership roles and responsibilities. It was preparing them not only for life as an adult, but it was equipping them for the tough days ahead and the struggles they would face.

It was through this association that I came to know Daisy Bates. She and her husband mentored me, and I admired what they were trying to do. It didn't take long for Mrs. Bates to put me to work as one of her lieutenants. I was one of her conduits to the younger members of the NAACP and those on college campuses.

On May 17, 1954, the U.S. Supreme Court delivered a stinging blow to the notion of "separate but equal" education in America. Everyone knew that black schools were underfunded and that dark-skinned students suffered as a result of substandard facilities and supplies. The high court affirmed that which was common knowledge by issuing a unanimous opinion that "in the field of public education the doctrine of 'separate but equal' has no place". Thus, the decision was made to desegregate the schools across the country. We knew that in Little Rock this proposition would be met with resistance by whites. It is one thing to make a law, but yet another thing to enforce it. Arkansas would not go along easily, nor did countless other school districts across the country.

It was up to the NAACP to ensure that the state of Arkansas enforced this national ruling. Three years after desegregation became the law of the land, the Little Rock School Board announced it would comply with the ruling. The question now was who will go?

Central High School was to be the testing ground for this decision. This would not be an easy task by any means. Daisy Bates knew that she would have to find just the right students to be the first to attend Central High. For years black students had been walking past Central to get to Dunbar. There was no bus service for black students, so the parents who had cars would drive their children to school or they would simply walk. Even that was risky because many times students were taunted by whites as they walked to class.

The plan was put into motion to find young soldiers who would make history at Central High School. We took several approaches to making this happen and we enlisted the help of two true human rights advocates and activists; Georg and Wilma Iggers, both professors at Philander Smith College. Georg G. Iggers was born Georg Gerson Igersheimer on December 7, 1926 in Hamburg, Germany.

Georg was raised in both the liberal and Orthodox Judaism. Life for him was frothed with challenges, and fears, much like African Americans in the deep south at the same time of his childhood. At age 10, he was asked by his friends to join the Junvolk, the pre-Hitler youth organization. Realizing his heritage, other friends encouraged him, and rightly so, to hide the fact that he was Jewish. Soon after that incident, Georg came face-to-face with anti-Semitism. While walking down the street one day, he saw a sign in a number of store windows, and in the movie theater, each of them reading the same thing, "Juden unerwunscht" or translated "Jews Not Wanted."

The hatred toward Jews had always existed, mostly just beneath the surface of this European City, but now it was printed on a sign and placed in full view for everyone to see. I did not have to imagine how this made my future friend feel. It reminds me of the "No Coloreds Allowed" or "Colored Served in Rear". And those were the polite signs announcing to everyone that Whites were only allowed in some public areas. There were others who told of the consequences of being in an all-white area after dark. Hatred – no matter to who it is directed is a vile and almost inhuman reaction. Yet the history of the world is replete with examples of human beings allowing fear to escalate into hate and hate into violence and violence into death.

In his youth, Georg was soon to experience this type of hatred even more. The threat of violence against this child who never hurt a soul was just beginning. He recalls with remarkable clarity his first real confrontation with those who despised him simply because of his heritage, his blood. Once while walking a familiar street in his hometown, he was confronted by boys about his age. They were wearing the uniforms of the Hitler Youth. They were armed with knives, and looking for Jews. They stopped him on a public street and threatened him. Both fear and anger began to swell in his young body, with fear overcoming anger when they made gestures that signaled an attack on his life. Instead, they pushed him down a flight of stairs and left his bruised body crumpled on a landing below.

A few days after his eleventh birthday in 1937, Georg's parents sent him to the Israelite Orphanage and Reformatory in Esslingen near Stuggart in southwest

Germany. They told him he was going on a vacation; instead he arrived at the reformatory that actually turned into a good experience for him. He learned more about his heritage and took classes in advance studies. It was actually a place of protection and learning and provided this inquisitive young man with a passion not only for learning, but for using his learnedness to bring about change.

Outside the reformatory, life for Jews was getting worse. Hitler's armies were growing. His followers were becoming more vocal. Georg's family saw the danger intensify and decided it was time to leave. With very little money the Igersheimers left all they owned behind and escaped what would surely result in sudden death. Georg recalls with clarity of anyone who has been the target of a life-threatening experience. It is not something anyone forgets and years later peculiar sights and smells and sounds can trigger memories long repressed by time and space.

"We could not have left at a better time, because on November 9, 1938 there was the tragic event known as Kristallnacht or "Crystal Night," Georg told me years later. On this dreadful night, more than 8,000 Jewish homes and shops were ransacked by storm troopers. The soldiers destroyed neighborhoods with sledge-hammers. The windows of many homes were made of crystal. But the beautiful glass littered the streets thus bringing about the name of this devastation – "Night of Broken Glass." Many of the people were dragged into the streets and beaten to death. Synagogues were set on fire.

"It was the beginning of the Holocaust. The plan to exterminate the Jews was underway." Georg and his family had left their home five weeks earlier. The day after the carnage began he arrived in the United States. Their thoughts were of their friends and relatives who had not escaped. In reflection on this period of his life Georg said, "Surely our leaving was a miracle. Had we not left when we did we most certainly would have died at Auschwitz." Auschwitz was the most notorious of all the Nazi death camps. Jewish prisoners were brought by the train carloads to the concentration camp in Poland. They were separated into three different camps – each with the same intent and purpose, to demean, and eventually kill.

The saddest of all were the children. Some of them were much younger than Georg. More than two hundred thirty-two thousand infants and children were held at Auschwitz. Many of them were used in horrible medical experiments that ended with their death – some by lethal injection. Georg escaped from this – but it no doubt haunts him that others did not, perhaps some he knew.

Upon arriving in the United States, Georg's family met with an agency that helped Jewish families relocate to the U.S. Georg was educated in private and public schools and eventually enrolled in college in Richmond, Virginia. He married Wilma and together they sought teaching jobs. They were readily accepted at historically black colleges because there was a dire need for professors in all aspects of education. They eventually landed in Little Rock on the campus of my alma mater, Philander Smith. This was to be a perfect match, two well-rounded and traveled educators and a liberal arts college in need of more PhD professors. It was the summer of 1950, and I had just received my undergraduate degree. The Iggers were moved into housing on the campus in a small shotgun house made of clapboard, resting on brick blocks. They lived at 1116 Izard Street among black people who welcomed them with open arms. At the time, the only other PhD educator on campus was Dr. Marquis Lafayette Harris, the president of Philander Smith. Dr. Harris was quite an educator and administrator who went on to become a bishop in the Methodist Church. During his tenure at Philander Smith, Dr. Harris was determined to make the little school matter. It was important to him to make education relevant and just as vital as the mighty halls of the Ivy League. After all, the students represented more than just another group of students seeking a degree. They were the hope of a people. This generation was on the cusp of incredible change in this nation and their contributions were important. These young minds were the offspring of a generation of people who had endured some of the darkest days of African-American history. Their parents and grandparents were just a generation away from slavery. They heard the stories, saw tears and experienced the fear. Dr. Harris saw that in each of these students. He realized his responsibility to them, their families and their futures. The colleges that educated Blacks gave them knowledge, hope and a mandate for change. Philander Smith did not disappoint them. It fulfilled that requirement and then some.

That was quite a goal, especially since most of the students were poor, and arrived on Dr. Harris' campus with varying levels of abilities and knowledge. Some went to school a few months out of the year and had to work in the fields the rest of the time. Others came from school systems that faced a lack of books and supplies, under-trained teachers and a school administration that cared little for black children. But they were important at Philander Smith. Marquis Lafayette Smith wanted them to succeed, and under his direction many students, including me, did.

The Iggers were no strangers to this concept. They arrived on campus at a dramatic time of transition for the education system in Little Rock. Professor Iggers was appalled at the conditions under which students had to learn, especially since things were so different for white students, both on the college campuses and in the public schools.

In the spring of 1952, Dr. Iggers studied the inequalities between the two public high schools in Little Rock. He compared teaching conditions at the all-black Dunbar High School and the all-white Little Rock Senior High, which was renamed Central High School. Little Rock Senior High School had a capacity of 3,000 students, but it had an enrollment of only 1,438. Meanwhile, Dunbar was built to accommodate 1,600 students, but it was overcrowded because the 1,525 senior high school students shared the building with the junior high school and a junior college.

There was a lack of classrooms for study halls. Three to four hundred students were required to be in the auditorium during their study periods. Three classes met in the cafeteria where the band also practiced and interfered with instruction. Because of the lack of space – classes were only forty-two minutes each while at Little Rock – classes ran for fifty-five minutes.

The library was so small at Dunbar teachers were advised to issue only two or three permits an hour for use of the library while students at Little Rock Senior High school could use theirs freely. In addition to Little Rock Senior High School, there was a special technical high school. There was no special instruction at Dunbar, just the core requirements.

I knew this information all too well and had been among those crowded into Dunbar. I still felt like I received a good education to the credit of a dedicated group of teachers who were well aware of their circumstance. They believed a person must make do with what he or she has. This has been our legacy throughout life – to make a way out of no way – to rise to the occasion in the face of difficulty and adversity. Teachers taught. We had few discipline problems and issues that did arise were dealt with and we moved on.

We had a sense of excitement and apprehension when the decision was made to finally integrate the schools. Separate but equal was about to be a thing of the past. Getting to that point would be the problem. Our greatest feat would be to get white families and white teachers to integrate black faces into their previously all-white environments. We would even face opposition from the governor himself.

Schools across the country were making attempts at becoming integrated. They faced issues, but the process moved along and people eventually accepted the change, except for in the South. Some school districts did not try to camouflage their discontent and fought vehemently against the move, including Arkansas.

The NAACP held countless meetings to discuss the integration concept and the school board's plan. Daisy Bates was bound and determined to make it work.

We were told Governor Faubus had planned to stand between black students and their education. White groups organized and protested from the state capitol to the high school campus. Even amid those protests, we continued to put a plan into action. The first task was finding the students to take the first steps and enroll for the fall semester. We would first need to choose students who had good grades and were even tempered and willing to be the first.

In this particular case Wilma and Georg Iggers were our means of getting school records that had been off limits to blacks. Professor Iggers approached the school board and asked to see the records under the pretense of doing research for his doctoral degree, a degree he had earned some time earlier. The school board was eager to help and allowed him and Wilma unfettered access to any documents they needed. Their mission was to review the records of black students and select those with the best grades and the greatest potential for learning.

While those tasks were being performed, I joined a small group of NAACP members who literally went door to door interviewing students and their parents. We were broken up into four teams of three. This was going to be a tough sell. Many of the black families earned their salary from white employers who were not keen on the idea of integration. So rather than jeopardize their earnings and possibly their jobs, many parents opted not to participate. Some of them feared that by becoming a part of this movement, their families would be harmed by those who would intimidate the students. We were in the streets almost every day mingling with the families and searching for candidates for the integration push. A number of families were ready and willing to participate. Many of them were employed by the school system, and we felt those students should not be included in fear of retaliation against their parents.

As I talked with those mothers and fathers, I could see the apprehension in their faces. I heard it in their voices. They knew the reality and the gravity of this situation. Some of them had come to Little Rock from other rural areas and had been witness to the terror rained on blacks. They saw the lynchings. They had seen the homes firebombed and cowered in their homes when the Klan came riding through. They had escaped that life and moved to a bigger town where there were greater numbers of blacks in larger neighborhoods. They had sought the safety in numbers and had started a new life. They were not about to risk their lives and the lives of their children. I knew there would be those who felt this way. I knew there would be some who felt just the opposite. They would jump at the chance to make this happen. They were not always the best candidates. We could ill afford an unbridled student or a rebellious family. That would thwart our purpose and possibly bring harm to other students and put a chilling effect on the effort. We had to find the right ones. We knew they were in Little Rock. We knew we would find them.

It was more about bringing change for these families. But rather, it was about bringing change for my family. After all, I was a father and my daughters were a part of the school system in Little Rock. My daughter, Angela, was interviewed by the school board. Angela was well aware of what might happen should she be asked to walk among those crowds and into Central High School. She has always been a playful, yet high-spirited child. Also, she was never at a loss for words. Angela was asked how she would respond to any acts of violence against her during this process. She was honest and forthright in her response. She looked the interviewer straight in the eye. She even raised her voice just a little and said, "If anyone kicks me, I will kick them back". Surprised at the answer, the interviewer quickly wrapped up the session and made quick notes on Angela. She was clearly not the right one to be put to the test of a hostile mob.

The plan was coming together nicely and we were informed of the school board's phase-in plan for integrating the schools. The first phase would begin in the 1957-58 school year with the senior high schools participating, including grades ten through twelve. After that phase was completed to the satisfaction of the board, then the junior high schools would be integrated and finally the elementary schools would be included.

Seventeen students were chosen by the school board based in part on our recommendations. These were to be the ones who made history in this racially-divided town. However, some of them lost their nerve and the numbers began to drop. By the fall of 1957 the number was down to nine – The Little Rock Nine.

A group of white residents vehemently against school integration formed the "Mothers League of Little Rock Central High School". Very few of the members of this movement actually had students attending Central High School. Local government leaders claimed the "troubles" were caused by "outside influences". But yet a group of people who didn't have children in school, and some of whom were from outside the area were allowed to protest an issue that did not directly affect them.

On August 27, 1957, a lawsuit was filed in Chancery Court by Mrs. Clyde A. Thomason. She requested an injunction to delay the start of integration. Mrs. Thomason testified she had been told that the mothers were terrified to send their children to Central High because of a rumor that the white and Negro youths were forming gangs and some of them were armed with guns and knives. Thomason's biggest supporter was the governor. He backed those claims, but neither mentioned a source of their information. Federal Judge Ronald

Davies granted the injunction which was soon overruled by a federal judge. There is an interesting twist to the efforts to integrate the schools and it came from an unlikely source. There were some black families who were against integration and warned the nine not to go. These were not bad people, to the contrary, these were people who were afraid – concerned about their own safety and the security of their jobs. Many of them were employed by white businesses and their bosses were against integration. Some were even pressured by their employees to speak out against the movement in hopes of stopping the inevitable. This instilled fear came with it the stark and sobering reality that if those who were intimidated did not speak out against the movement, they very well could have lost their jobs. Their better judgment was tempered by notion that they could no longer care for their families and could have been blacklisted from other jobs as well.

Black families and their black neighbors engaged in heated debates against each other. Nine students were in a quandary feeling as if they had somehow brought about this controversy. But that was far from the case. They were informed of such, which helped to steel their resolve. They were not to be turned around. They were prepared for what was ahead, or so they thought they were. There was no real way to prepare them for what they would experience. They knew of the potential violence and were aware that even the governor was against it, but their own people had planted a seed of doubt.

We were now 24 hours away from the attempt to integrate Central High School on the first day of the school year. With a calm exterior fortified by steeled nerves, the nine were prepared for their first steps into history. It was September 2, 1957 and while final preparations were underway, we received word that the Arkansas National Guard had surrounded Central High School. Governor Faubus went on television to explain his actions.

"Units of the National Guard have been and are now being mobilized with the mission to maintain or restore the peace and good order of this community. Advance units are already on the grounds of Central High School."

He said he had heard that white supremacists from all over the state were heading to Little Rock. He made the declaration that Central High School was to be off limits to all blacks and the all-black high school would be off limits to whites. I could not believe the audacity of this man – the governor of the state of Arkansas – making the proclamation that if black students attempted to enter Central High School, "blood would run in the streets." Faubus had been considered a moderate and had been elected by in no small part the black voting public. He had been chosen over a known segregationist. Faubus made his statements to make people believe he was trying to prevent violence. But in fact, his sole purpose was to prevent these students from entering school.

I have always been amazed that those in power seek to keep people powerless through fear and intimidation. Orval Faubus was seeking re-election and thought he could score points by taking a stand against the federal government and the courts. He had no idea what he was doing to the reputation of his city and his state. All the eyes of the nation were focused on this town and on the young people who were to break the barrier.

The actions of the governor delayed the beginning of integration at Central High School. The black students were held up – disappointed but not dismayed as they watched white students once again walk into "their school". Instead they stayed home.

Two days later, Daisy Bates made the call to each of the students. They were to meet a few blocks from the school and then walk together to the school. As I remember it Elizabeth Eckford did not have a phone so she did not get the call. Instead, Elizabeth started to walk to the school on her own. When she got to the school, she was met by the mobs who had gathered in the streets, prepared to block the way of the students. Elizabeth walked on – all alone. She was attacked and threatened with lynching. The National Guard was there, but they did not intercede. The uniformed National Guard soldiers who were sworn to protect the nation from forces, foreign and domestic, just stood there and did not protect the young girl who simply wanted to go to school. I have often wondered what was going through their minds. Were they afraid? These men in uniform who could not profess a side, who could not make a move without orders, who could be called into battle in a far away land did not protect the least of these. Instead, they stood there and followed the orders of the governor and told Elizabeth she could not enter the school.

Elizabeth turned to talk walk away, but the hecklers in the mob would take turns stepping into her path. She turned and walked in another direction. Elizabeth had so looked forward to this day. She spent the better part of the summer making a new dress, was wearing new shoes and had her hair done perfectly. Instead, she was turned away and was subjected to near torture. At one point, she looked directly into the eyes of a white woman who was standing on the sidewalk. In an instant this woman spat in her face.

Reporters from around the country were there and tried to ask her questions. She remained silent and was confused. She wondered where were the other students who were supposed to join her. She found a place near the bus stop and sat down. The mobs continued to taunt her. A tear began to stream down her face from behind her large sunglasses. A reporter from a New York paper was there and moved in. He placed his arm around her and told her, "Don't let them see you cry." She wiped the tear from her face and then the mob turned on the reporter, threatening him. A kind face finally emerged from the crowd, a white woman yelled at the crowd, "This is a child, leave her alone!" She put her arm around Elizabeth and led her away. Elizabeth soon rejoined the group who had heard the commotion and inched forward toward the school. The remaining eight by now had reached the entrance to the school and they too were denied access to Little Rock High.

Hundreds of miles away President Dwight David Eisenhower was monitoring the events of the day. The White House had people there in the crowd who reported back to the President. It didn't take long for Eisenhower to make a move. In the meantime, Faubus was making claims the federal government was tapping his phones and secretly gathering information on him and his administration.

At the time, the President was at the U.S. Naval Base in Newport, Rhode Island. He quickly dispatched a telegram to Orval Faubus and followed it with the following letter:

The Honorable Orval E. Faubus
Governor of Arkansas
Little Rock, Arkansas

Your telegram received requesting my assurance of understanding of and cooperation in the course of action you have taken on school integration recommended by the Little Rock School Board and ordered by the United States District Court pursuant to the man-date of the United States Supreme Court.

When I became President, I took an oath to support and defend the Constitution of the United States. The only assurance I can give you is that the Federal Constitution will be upheld by me by every legal means at my command.

There is no basis of fact to the statements you make in your telegram that Federal authorities have been considering taking you into custody or that telephone lines to your Executive Mansion have been tapped by any agency of the Federal Government.

At the request of Judge Davies, the Department of Justice is presently collecting facts as to your interference with or failure to comply with the District Court's order. You and other state officials – as well as the National Guard, which, of course is uniformed, armed and partially sustained by the Government – will, I am sure, give full cooperation to the United States District Court.

– Dwight D. Eisenhower

With a single phone call hundreds of soldiers were mobilized. Already on alert, the 101st Airborne Division, the most elite fighters in the world, were called to action and arrived amid the turmoil in Little Rock, Arkansas. This fighting unit had been in wars and battles known and unknown, but yet they were in their own country prepared to carry out the orders of their Commander-In-Chief. The power of the 101st trumped the Arkansas National Guard. Armed and prepared to protect, American soldiers took up posts and cleared the way for nine unarmed soldiers whose sacrifice was heard around the world.

The presence of the 101st did not quell the hatred. From behind the barricade, the white mob threw something more painful than any stone. They yelled racial slurs and threats vowing the nine would not live and that their families would be harmed. The President of the United States, the most powerful leader in the world, could not stop the hatred of hundreds of his own citizens who tried to turn the tide of history and defy a law of the land. President Eisenhower assigned a personal guard to each of the students. They walked behind the students and escorted them to class. They stood in hallways and classrooms, protecting the nine.

Other black students were also the target of hatred. White students would walk up behind black children and step on the backs of their heels, pushing their shoes off their feet. When they kneeled to tie their shoes, they were surrounded, kicked and beaten. The boys were always the target of beatings by boys and men twice their size. Some of the black students went to class in torn clothes and bloodied heels from the attacks. But they would not be turned around. Black parents and other interested adults could only stand outside the schools worried about what was happening behind those bricked walls. The fear extended from the schools to the neighborhoods. Some black families remained against integration and made their voices heard. There was a lot of, "I told you this would happen!" There were skirmishes near the neighborhoods and threats called into homes. Residents would stand guard and watch their streets while nervous families slept inside.

One young woman named Melba Patillo was attacked by a mob who threw lighted dynamite sticks at her. Acid was thrown in her face. Had it not been for the 101st soldiers who saw what happened, she would have been killed. Instead these soldiers quickly washed her face and body in cold water, trying to flush the acid away. Their quick action saved her life and her sight.

From the safety of their homes, all across America – people watched history unfold on television. What they saw was the best and the worst of America. They witnessed the innocent, brave, and tormented. They also saw anger, hate, misunderstanding, and violence. Somewhere in the midst of all of that was the confused; those who didn't know what to think. This was the case throughout much of the Civil Rights Movement. There would always be those who would be on the fence. They knew in their heart of hearts things needed to change. There were those who were well intentioned – but were afraid to speak out, to step forward, to be heard and counted. There would forever be those whose silence was just as dangerous and damaging as those whose vile retorts were heard with a deafening clarity. I never fully understood that. I never could understand how anyone could see another person mistreated, hated and reviled and never speak out. I could never comprehend how a person could stand by and not make a sound, not offer help, and not try to make a difference. These were people who were afraid for their comfort to be disturbed. They were concerned that their making noise would threaten their way of life. They had the ability and the responsibility to speak, but they never said a mumbling word.

As the events in Little Rock unfolded, I began to wonder more about America. I was proud to be from Arkansas, but I was ashamed of the view America had of my state. I needed to be a voice with something to say and something to do.

A television audience saw human rage at its worst. I wondered what the people sitting in their darkened living rooms with only the glow of the television set were thinking of the mobs of people on both sides. While I admired those brave students and those of us who kept them going, I knew their popularity was tainted by the doubts of some of their own people. It would be the same for Martin Luther King Jr. and legions of other civil rights supporters who tried to make a difference, to bring about change. Change would not come easily. The most difficult change – was the change in the mind. A new course of thinking does not happen easily for anyone, especially when the safety and security of their children are at stake. There was the stark reality of the cost of these actions. There was no ignoring that people could and would be hurt. Lives would and could be lost, but never should efforts be halted because of the unpopularity of their actions. There was the future to think about – not just in Little Rock, but all across the country. The school system was for many communities a first step. Integration would play a bigger role in the overall movement than many people would realize. If only we could get these children to learn together, to play together, to be the catalyst for a change that would affect not just their lives but the lives of their parents and the lives of those children who would follow. I often thought about the other kids, those who were not part of the nine. I wondered would these actions change their image of integration and what would lie ahead for them.

Still in Little Rock – on streets where black families, lived there was the belief that what was being done was wrong and maybe segregation was not so bad. After all, in the black schools everyone knew everyone, crowded as it was; there was some comfort in knowing that there was a common interest, a common bond. However, it was hard to ignore the fact that separate was not equal and that the crowded conditions at black schools would not afford our students the kind of education to which they were entitled.

While these attempts at Central High continued, each day I would return to my home and my little girls. I would watch them play in the yard and talk with their friends. They were keenly aware of what was happening. Every morning they would stand in the yard of our home and watch the soldiers from the 82nd Airborne Division as they would march toward the school. They would look at them and would wave and smile. My little girls were not afraid, but instead were more intrigued. I would talk with them about what was going on. They would listen and their young minds seemed to understand. They understood that they were safe from harm, but they also knew that there were those who put themselves in harms way because the cause was greater than them. These brave people knew they were making life better for the long run and that these troubled days would end.

In many ways that is true about most anything worth fighting for. Some people cower away from tough assignments in fear of the unknown. They worry about themselves and families, and sometimes forget about the legions of others who will follow. They forget about those who will take up where they left off and who will not forget the sacrifice of the few for the benefit of the many.

It was a relatively calm, but uneasy day after a second night of rioting in the city. Rioters were triggered by a police action that was perceived by blacks to be an act of police brutality. Several shootings of black males had occurred prior to this situation causing high racial tension.

A white police officer came to the Dunbar Community Center, a regular hangout for young people. The officer came to arrest a young man for a minor infraction of the law. He found the young man outside on the basketball court engaged in a pickup game. When the officer tried to place the young man under arrest, he quickly found himself surrounded by nearly 20 of the teenagers who had gathered at the center. The officer drew his weapon and demanded that he and his prisoner be allowed to pass.

The young people held their ground and refused to allow the officer to leave. Sensing the danger for both the officer and the young people, I stepped into the middle of the circle. The look on the officer's face was certainly one of fear. What a dangerous combination, a white police officer with shaky hands and a loaded revolver, and angry group of young people. The officer had no portable radio to his base or his precinct and had no way to communicate with fellow officers that he was in trouble.

I looked at both the officer and the young people. I said to them all, "Look, let's make sure no one here does anything foolish. I am asking this officer to walk out of here without making an arrest. I am going to walk him to his car and you are going to let both of us leave." The officer was not impressed and said "I am not leaving here without the person I came to arrest." I emphasized to the officer his predicament and urged him to walk out of the circle with me. A young person yelled out, "Who told you we are going to let either of you go?"

Then there was a calmer voice in the crowd. A young man said, "Wait everybody, do you know who this is?" I was relieved – thinking the young man would tell them about my civil rights record. This was not to be. I was, however surprised by his next statement. "This is Mr. Sutton. He is the father of Angela Sutton. You remember Angela, she is in our English class. This is her father."

It was not what I expected, but it worked. I walked the officer to his car and he left – never to return – and never to make an arrest – at least not on that night.

Throughout this period of crisis, there were bonds that grew stronger under the strain of the moment. Friendships were made and others were strengthened. Such was the case on one of the days that the Little Rock Nine actually made it into class.

Our job was to get the students into the school unmolested as best we could. On this particular day, I was assigned to take up post on the steps of Central High School as a decoy. When white people saw black faces, that is all they saw. They did not distinguish between the faces of the students and those who were the supporters. To the white mob, we were all the same. So, when I went to the front steps of Central High School, the protesters thought I was one of the students. And quickly they began to surround me. The words coming out of their mouths were stinging. The hate dripping from their lips, the fire in their eyes, the clinched fists, were the result of weeks of just getting mad about integration and the promise to stop it from happening.

Their faces were so close to mine. I could feel the warmth of their breath and feel the spittle falling on my face. I decided to leave, to make a run for it and get away. I made it away from the front steps, but I turned around and saw a familiar face. It was that of Earl Davy, a reporter for the local paper. Davy was just behind me and as I was leaving two men attacked Davy. Their pent up rage unleashed on him with a fury. He was just there doing his job, taking photographs of the history unfolding before his Graflex lens. But these men were intent on disrupting by any possible means. They pushed Davy to the ground and smashed his camera. I could not let this happen. I turned without hesitation and went back into the carnage I had run from seconds ago. If I did not get to him, he would surely be seriously injured or killed. Davy looked up at me and said, "Ozell, what are you doing? They will kill us!"

I yelled back at him, "Not if we keep moving, now come on. I will not come back again!" Huddled together we shielded our heads and faces and took the punches and slaps as they landed all over us, but we kept moving till we made it away from the violence. We stood there for a moment and looked back and realized how close we had come to possibly losing our lives.

At this point in my life, I had been a U.S Marine. I had seen and heard gunfire. I was raised a brave man. However, there is no way to adequately describe human rage. It's something you will never forget. You will never forget the look of torment and anger that can gather in the face of a human being. I could not understand how people created in God's image could hate others who were created in the same way. I often wondered what Lula Belle would think about this rage, this hatred, so many years since times were "supposed to change". I guess she would stick to being Lula Belle and tell her son to continue to do right, to treat others right, to look up to no man and down on none. She always urged me to look every man in the eye, as an equal, a brother. But that's difficult to do when the man you are looking at wants to kill you simply because of the color of your skin. It amazes me that through all I have seen, and experienced, I never let hate creep into my body. Of course, I have been angry, upset and mad, but never had I hated a person. Once hate enters the heart, it can stay there and it grows. If you don't release it at some point, it will fester and develop into something that can launch out of control. In the days ahead, I would see hate over and over again and each time, I would hold on to the peace within me. I hoped others would see it and allow peace to control their thoughts and deeds.

The beating I took by the mob was my first in my quest for civil rights. Each and every blow was vivid. I carry with me the thought that I was taking those licks not for myself, but for those who would follow. I was not imaging that while it was happening. My thoughts would turn simply to survival and making it through. But after it was over, I realized this was just the beginning because there would be those who would at all cost try to stop the movement, the effort of forward progress. Of course, I would never want to be beaten again, but I would gladly stand up to the mobs if it would make a difference and improve the quality of life for people.

Those terrible days at Central High School would be recorded in the history books. It would serve as the proving ground for an expanded effort throughout the country to give black children a chance at an equal education and equal protection under the law. The people who played pivotal roles – the development of this chapter in history – would take their place in the minds of those who were there and those would read about it decades later.

Governor Faubus would be remembered as the one who had the power to make things right, but instead gave in to his weaker side. He desired to keep things the way they were and deny black children a good education and the hope of equality. Many would say Faubus thrust the state of Arkansas into an unfavorable light and other politicians would learn from his mistakes.

Daisy Bates would go down in history as more than a champion for civil rights. She would continue to make good on the promises of the constitution and the laws of the land. She would be heralded as a journalist, an activist, a community leader, and a woman of God. Her right hand, L.C., would be right there.

President Eisenhower would be remembered as a statesman who used the power of his office to enforce not just the laws, but to guarantee the protection of citizens. This former army general knew how to fight and he knew that, at times, fighting was a necessary evil. It came with the territory of the presidency and the awesome responsibility of serving as the leader of the free world. That phrase, "free world," sounds strange in context to the struggle. Free men and women living in "the free world," were being held hostage by the fears of a few.

Once the nine were in school, President Eisenhower did not abandon them. Members of the 101st Airborne division remained for weeks in Little Rock. The mobs had become resigned to the fact that the students were in school and there was no turning back. They were there to stay. But staying in school was a task in and of itself. Once inside the school, the students were subject to horrible treatment. The soldiers from Fort Bragg could only do so much. The nine would have to get along as best they could. They had to constantly wipe their faces of spit spewed from the mouths of the white students. They were the targets of relentless hazing at the hands of a few white students. Some teachers refused to educate these children in the same manner they taught white students. In fact, some black students were not taught at all in some classes, they were just there, alone, ostracized by their fellow students and now their teachers.

We anticipated this type of treatment and had a plan to help the students each and every step. These students had a great many resources at their disposal. They had access to the entire campus of Philander Smith College. The professors there were available to help the students with their classes. Georg Iggers and I organized tutoring sessions with the students and helped them with lessons and homework.

We would meet on Saturdays with the students to discuss with them about the previous week and prepare them for every possible scenario. Their presence at Little Rock High School would be a challenge for the entire school year. We taught them ways to avoid confrontation and how to prevent being a victim of attacks. The students were instructed to never enter a bathroom alone. They would use the buddy system. They were instructed to always walk down the middle of the hallway to avoid being pushed up against the walls. The hecklers would sometimes force them up against the lockers and surround them so no one could see their quick punches or them being knocked to the floor.

The nine students took the punches, but they didn't like it. When they were knocked down, they got up. When they faced obstacles, they walked around them and at the end of the day they went home. Each day was a gift. Each day was a challenge – a challenge they met with dignity and the pride in knowing their struggle was for every other Negro child who simply wanted to learn. I admired the bravery of these young souls. They never talked about quitting, though it was sometimes evident in their eyes. They never uttered a word, but instead they endured the pain in silence and often in solitude. Along the way people would keep them encouraged because they too, knew the value of the sacrifice of the nine students who changed history. It was my blessing to be there. It was their fortitude that continued to strengthen me for the battles that would lie ahead. And just like them, I would not be moved.

Arkansas Council on Human Relations

"Then I said, I will not make mention of him, nor speak any more in his name. But his word was in mine heart as a burning fire shutup in my bones, and I was weary with forbearing, and I could not stay."
— Jeremiah 20:9

I can't imagine what Jeremiah, an Old Testament Bible prophet in the Bible, went through in his troubled life, but I can identify with his issue with the Lord. He wanted to put the word of his God almighty out of his mind, but he couldn't. When he tried, it continued to torment him and to keep his soul at uneasy. It burned like a fire all shut up in his bones.

The next couple of years were dedicated to taking care of my family and maintaining an alert ear to the progress of my people in Little Rock. I went back to WinRock out of necessity and continued my job there for more than a year. While I was there, more than 50 miles from the city, living in luxury, I knew there were those who were in need and mired in the ugliness of discrimination. This haunted me. It vexed me so that there were times when I started to move right back and continue with the struggle.

For me, being involved with the crisis at Central High School was like the fuel that runs a car. The circumstances of those days continued to course through my veins days after the dust had settled in the hallways of Central. I did not wonder if I would continue, but how. I knew the die had been cast for me and that my calling was continued service to people and to pursue the cause of human rights wherever the need would arise. I didn't have to look far because there were so many inequities.

I eventually left Winrock, but maintained a great relationship and friendship with the Rockefellers. I had always been told when you leave a job, leave on good terms, never burn a bridge that you may have to one day go back across. There was never a reason for me to be unhappy with the Rockefeller family. Although they were my employers, they always treated me with respect and dignity, and always extended that level of caring to my family as well.

The Rockefellers understood my consternation and did not hesitate to allow me to return to Little Rock. I needed to be close to the roots of the movement. In 1958, I left to assume a job with the Little Rock Housing Authority. I began work as a relocation supervisor, a position I would hold for one year. It was my job to assist residents who were being moved because of urban renewal. The people I was responsible for were very poor; their homes were nothing more than shacks, wooden shotgun houses that sometimes sat on cinder blocks. The area was being gentrified, made into better housing, housing these people could not afford. It was quite clear to me that when these people left their homes, they would likely not return to the area. It was the way of America, a practice that exists in cities large and small. Older housing is destroyed for something newer and more appealing to people who would otherwise not live there. Consequently, the complexion of the neighborhoods would change as well. Black neighborhoods became all-white, and in the years to follow the complexion would change again. This was a practice with which I was most uncomfortable. Many of the people who lived in these neighborhoods had been there for generations. They had been poor. We were now about to make matters worse. City and state officials offered to purchase their houses and their land at "fair market value." This was far less than what new housing would cost, so they were forced to rent, move into the housing projects or leave the city. I grew frustrated with the system. I could not bear to tell these good hard-working people they were about to lose everything. They had no choice, but they were facing this grim reality. They were going to move and the state or the city would possess their land. After all, they would have to say goodbye to the place where they raised their children and said goodbye to their parents. It was the place where they celebrated many holidays, birthdays, and graduations. It was the place where they had endured hard suffering, yet maintained a faithful belief and hope for a better day. Their tears and sorrows had all been contained within the walls of their homes they were to lose forever. How could I continue to do this? I simply could not. After a year, I left the job and did not return.

In one of my many conversations with Mrs. Rockefeller, she convinced me to return to Petit Jean Mountain to serve as the public affairs coordinator for special events at the estate. I assisted in planning major parties and events at the cattle business. My entire family was moved to the estate. We were provided with a house that was fully furnished with the Rockefeller's surplus furniture. There were fine paintings and linens in our home. The chef in the main house prepared our meals and the same maids who cared for the mansion also serviced our home. Groundskeepers tended the yards and kept beautiful flowers for us just as they did all over the grounds of WinRock. Joanna maintained a teaching job not far from the estate and our girls went to school near where Joanna taught.

For two years, we lived in luxury, but my soul did not. Again I was tormented with the knowledge that while I enjoyed the beauty and the splendor of this life, there were those who barely could make it and in doing so they were mistreated and abused and denied access to those things whites took for granted. I had to go back. I had to continue that which I started. I had to return to Little Rock.

I discussed this with Joanna and while she understood my dilemma, she was not sympathetic. She thought I was crazy for leaving this good job and moving our family back to the city. Deep in her heart though, Joanna was of like mind and spirit. Her focus was and always has been our family. She also realized that what affects other families affects us. She was a great support in my times of trepidation and eventually acquiesced to my yearning for involvement in the movement. Joanna had faith in me, though I never was one who needed a great deal of support. I always believed in me, even when others did not. However, it was important to me that my helpmate be supportive of my cause. She knew that the life at WinRock was artificial. It was unlike the lives of those who lived in other parts of the state. We were living a good life. We enjoyed it there, but we knew the time had come to go and to take up our rightful place in the grassroots effort to set things right.

When we moved back to Little Rock, we had a difficult time finding adequate housing. We ended our search by deciding to rent a small house. We quickly realized how good life was at WinRock. We had grown accustomed to the luxury of central heat and air conditioning. We now suffered through the Arkansas summers like so many families who were without air. I was quickly reminded of where I was, who I was and the personal resources I had available to me.

I applied for and was hired for a job with one of the organizations that was dedicated to the same causes for which I had pledged my life, the Arkansas Council on Human Relations (ACHR). I was hired as an associate director.

The ACHR was founded in December 1954. Like most organizations, it was formed out of a need, specifically to shepherd the desegregation of public facilities including schools, restaurants, businesses, and the government itself. There was a need to keep government officials accountable when it came to implementing and maintaining laws against discrimination.

In his paper, "Facilitating Change: The Arkansas Council on Human Relations, 1954-1964," John Kirk of the Royal Holloway & Bedford College at the University of London, described the mission of ACHR:

"The ACHR provided an important hub of communication between blacks and whites throughout a period of racial polarization. It provided moral and legal support for school officials at a time of crisis. It exerted pressure on white community leaders to embrace peaceful racial change. It nurtured local black leaders and organi-

zations by providing positions of leadership responsibility and acting as a forum for inter- as well as intra-racial contact. It provided a vital bridge between national and regional organizations within the civil rights movement and those at a local level. With few resources and little fanfare, the ACHR's seemingly modest goals actually placed it many times at the heart of the process of racial change in Arkansas."

ACHR was four years old when I began working with it. I was still a relatively young man and went to work right away with young people. I educated them on the current status of the movement and the areas where ACHR could help. There was no shortage of people interested in making a difference, both black and white. The terrible days of Orval Faubus had in many ways galvanized the resolve of people of goodwill. Arkansans had suffered through the embarrassment of having their state plastered in the newspaper headlines and in the same sentences with words like racism, discrimination, and segregation. Television reports had shown the worst of Arkansas. People around the world saw the hatred on the faces of the mobs and they saw the fear etched on the faces of those who were attacked. The dark days of those few weeks had done a damage that would live on for decades. Of course, some people bore words of hatred like badges on a uniform. They wanted to send a message to those who would see it. They were just as determined to keep things as they were just as people like me were determined to bring about change.

The beauty of youth is that it fosters enthusiasm whether it is for a sport, love, or noble cause. This made the recruitment of young people not only easy, but very necessary. It seems that people tend to appreciate those things they work and sacrifice for – more than those things that come easily. As I maintained strong ties to my alma mater, Philander Smith continued to play a vital role in the cause of equal rights.

In the years to come students from this august body would be on the forefront of sit-ins and protests and large demonstrations. These young people would not only know bravery, but would demonstrate it time and time again. They would need it.

"Social Transition"

In a landmark speech by President John F. Kennedy, he addressed a much neglected issue in America: the equal treatment of the black citizens in all aspects of life, from the cradle to the grave.

The speech was prompted by the initial denial of admission of two Negro students to the University of Alabama. The most memorable moment of that era was Governor George Wallace symbolically standing in the doorway of a class-room building in the face of National Guard troops sent to escort the students in. It happened without violence, but Kennedy saw the bigger picture, the reluctance to accept fellow citizens, human beings as equals. This prompted what I think was the greatest speech Kennedy ever delivered. His words were my words. His thoughts were my thoughts. His mission was on a parallel course to my cause. He had the power to make it happen. I assumed the responsibility for making it happen. These excerpts from his televised speech on Tuesday, June 11, 1963 captured the essence of the need for the movement. It would also likely be the cause of Kennedy's death and the reason he is so revered among people of color.

"This Nation was founded by men of many nations and backgrounds. It was founded on the principle that all men are created equal, and that the rights of every man are diminished when the rights of one man are threatened. Today we are committed to a worldwide struggle to promote and protect the rights of all who wish to be free.

And when Americans are sent to Vietnam or West Berlin, we do not ask for whites only. It ought to be possible, therefore, for American students of any color to attend any public institution they select without having to be backed up by troops.

It ought to be possible for American consumers of any color to receive equal service in places of public accommodation, such as hotels and restaurants and theaters and retail stores, without being forced to resort to demonstrations in the street, and it ought to be possible for American citizens of any color to register and to vote in a free election without interference or fear of reprisal. It ought to be possible, in short, for every American to enjoy the privileges of being American without regard to his race or his color.

In short, every American ought to have the right to be treated as he would wish to be treated, as one would wish his children to be treated. But this is not the case.

The Negro baby born in America today, regardless of the section of the Nation in which he is born, has about one-half as much chance of completing a high school as a white baby born in the same place on the same day, one-third as much chance of completing college, one-third as much chance of becoming a professional man, twice as much chance of becoming unemployed, about one-seventh as much chance of earning $10,000 a year, a life expectancy which is seven years shorter, and the prospects of earning only half as much.

This is not a sectional issue. Difficulties over segregation and discrimination exist in every city, in every State of the Union, producing in many cities a rising tide of discontent that threatens the public safety. Nor is this a partisan issue. In a time of domestic crisis men of good will and generosity should be able to unite regardless of party or politics. This is not even a legal or legislative issue alone. It is better to settle these matters in the courts than on the streets, and new laws are needed at every level, but law alone cannot make men see right.

We are confronted primarily with a moral issue. It is as old as the scriptures and is as clear as the American Constitution. The heart of the question is whether all Americans are to be afforded equal rights and equal opportunities, whether we are going to treat our fellow Americans as we want to be treated.

If an American, because his skin is dark, cannot eat lunch in a restaurant open to the public, if he cannot send his children to the best public school available, if he cannot vote for the public officials who represent him, if, in short, he cannot enjoy the full and free life which all of us want, then who among us would be content to have the color of his skin changed and stand in his place? Who among us would then be content with the counsels of patience and delay?

One hundred years of delay have passed since President Lincoln freed the slaves, yet their heirs, their grandsons, are not fully free. They are not yet freed from the bonds of injustice. They are not yet freed from social and economic oppression. And this Nation, for all its hopes and all its boasts, will not be fully free until all its citizens are free.

We preach freedom around the world, and we mean it, and we cherish our freedom here at home, but are we to say to the world, and much more importantly, to each other that this is a land of the free except for the Negroes; that we have no second-class citizens except Negroes; that we have no class or caste system, no ghettoes, no master race except with respect to Negroes?

Now the time has come for this Nation to fulfill its promise."

Those words would ring in my ears and stir within me a passion that would burn for years to come. Many tears would shed, many a men would be beaten, and many lives would be lost. When Kennedy spoke, he was in actuality speaking his epitaph and writing his own obituary. For like so many people of the movement, he would work, but see no end to his work day. He would dream and never see it manifest. He would be brave, but die at the hands of a cowardly assassin.

It was a routine day for me save the fact that I was boarding an airplane for a trip to Houston. I had been invited to speak on the campus of Texas Southern University. Also, on the program that week was the great Barbara Jordan. Ever since I received word she would be attending the same conference, I prayed I would not have to follow her speech. There was no way I could hold a candle to that voice, to that mind, to that eloquent speaker. I have always thought I was good, but I am man enough to know when the best man for the job is a woman – especially if her name was Barbara Jordan. In addition to that, I was to speak on Barbara's home turf. She was a graduate of Texas Southern, an attorney and a much sought-after speaker, in particular from her sorority sisters of Delta Sigma Theta Sorority Inc. At that time, Jordan was considering a run for a seat in the Texas legislature. However, on this day, the presence of Barbara Jordan and Ozell Sutton would be dwarfed by an event that would change the course of Civil Rights. This day was November 22, 1963.

It was one hundred sixty-five days after John F. Kennedy had delivered that poignant speech. I arrived at the airport in Little Rock and while waiting to board the plane, the announcement was made in the airport. John F. Kennedy had been shot while in a motorcade in Dallas, Texas. The busy airport with people moving about from gate to gate came to a standstill. There was silence and there were tears followed by bowed heads and prayers for his recovery. I boarded the plane and we took off. Minutes into the flight the pilot delivered the news. John F. Kennedy was dead. Passengers and the flight crew were visibly shaken. People cried, some uncontrollably. I felt an emptiness followed by anger. How could they do this? The pilot had few details, but even his remorse was felt in his voice. It occurred to

Lula Belle Sutton

Ozell Sutton, USMC

NAACP Convention
Dr. Martin Luther King, Jr., March on Washington
Crowds at Lincoln Memorial

Ozell and Joanna
Ambassador Andrew Young & Ozell Sutton
Congressman Andrew Young & Mayor Maynard Jackson with Ozell Sutton

103

U.S. Attorney General Eric Holder, Former U.S. Attorney General Janet Reno, Ozell Sutton, CRS Staff
Ozell Sutton, Dr. Benjamin Hooks, Dr. William V. Guy at Friendship Baptist Church
Ozell speaks from the balcony of the Lorraine Motel

John Williams, Dr. Henry Ponder, Ozell Sutton, Vic Carter at the White House
Ozell Sutton & Rev. Jesse Jackson
President Bill Clinton and Ozell Sutton

Dick Gregory and Ozell Sutton

Ozell & Joanna
Afrika Jonee Prat-Ansa, Angela Cassandra Martin, Samuel Martin
Khalil Sutton (Not Pictured), Dietre Jo Sutton, Alta Phatena Sutton, Angela Cassandra Sutton

me that this was a murder, an attempt to stop a dream. Kennedy was killed and it was hoped that his thoughts and legislation would die with him. It did not. The Kennedy Civil Rights Bill was being debated before congress at the time of his death.

Moments after the president's death was confirmed, United States District Judge Sarah T. Hughes swore in the next President of the United States, then Vice President Lyndon B. Johnson. This had the civil rights community concerned because Johnson had a poor record on civil rights. But it was Johnson who pushed Kennedy's bill through. It was not without opposition. Johnson's friend and mentor Georgia Senator Richard B. Russell led the charge to block the legislation. He organized 18 southern democratic senators to filibuster the bill. This dragged on until June 1964 when the filibuster ended and the bill passed 73 to 27.

Johnson signed the Civil Rights Act on July 2, 1964. There is a widely believed rumor that once the bill was signed, Johnson told an aide, "We have lost the south for a generation." (The Boston Globe 2006-03-05)

This act made racial discrimination in public places illegal. It included places like theaters, restaurants, hotels, stores, etc. It also required employers to provide equal employment opportunities. It also provided for free access to participate in election, voting rights in public polling places.

It was a time of "social transition" that Martin Luther King, Jr. talked about so much. Laws had been passed banning discrimination in public places. The problem was that it had not been banished in the minds of all the people. This was a time of realization for some that their dreams of being able to enjoy simple rights were coming true. They would be able to shop where they wanted, drive where they wanted, live where they wanted and eat where they wanted. This would not come easy. Even some of the biggest businesses were not threatened by the law enacted by The Congress of the United States and signed by the president. They held on and refused to follow the mandates that sought to give hardworking, everyday people the same privileges that allowed for "the pursuit of happiness". It was the job of ACHR to be vigilant in pushing for compliance with those laws.

In my years with this agency, we met and worked with a number of businesses encouraging them to open their doors and their services to black people. Some of them complied willingly. Others needed some gentle persuasion. Many restaurant owners and operators refused to serve "coloreds." There was something obscene in the minds of whites when it came to one of the primary elements we all had in common; the need to sustain our lives with food. The breaking of bread in close proximity to Negroes seemed to be the last straw. Blacks might shop in the same places as Whites. Whites might now allow their children to go to school with Blacks. Whites might let Blacks on the buses, in the libraries or in the same parks, but some Whites were not about to sit down and eat off the same plates and forks that were used by Blacks. No way!

It was the same all across the south. We were tired of waiting. We wanted to be served at the lunch counters and in the restaurants and in the diners like everyone else. At the same time as ACHR took its stance via demonstrations another organization called the Student Non-violent Coordinating Committee, better known as SNCC, pronounced "snick." SNCC was founded on the campus of Shaw University in Raleigh, N.C. It was formulated to give college students an active voice in the movement that would determine their future. Some of the protests of students from SNCC received tremendous publicity and served as landmarks for other protests across the country. The most celebrated was that of four African-American students from Greensboro's Agricultural and Technical College. Franklin McCain, Joseph McNeil, David Richmond and Ezell A. Blair, Jr. defied posted signs and sat down to be served at a lunch counter at Woolworth's in downtown Greensboro. These men followed the teachings of Martin Luther King, and chose to protest nonviolently. Their story was captured by the media and it was beamed around the world.

Nearly at the same time, other students from other campuses took up similar causes in their hometowns. Little Rock, Arkansas was no exception. There were protests at some of this city's biggest businesses including Mclellums, Woolworth's and a store named Blass.

There was a pattern to the way the protests took place. Someone would go inside the establishment and try to be served. More often than not, they would be refused. One after one, day after day, we would test the restaurants to be sure this was a pattern in practice. We would compare notes and then a decision would be made whether to protest the proprietor. If the decision was yes, then people would have to be recruited to participate. They would have to know first of all the reason for the sit-in. They would have to be willing to be exposed to some of the most vile names they had ever been called. They also would have to be willing to break the law. In those days after you were ordered to leave a business, they would likely call the police and you would be arrested. You also had to be able to remain nonviolent and passive throughout the protest. Many times the other patrons would humiliate you, throw things at you, or simply pour their food on you. Through it all you had to maintain your calm, sit there and take it, and you had to be willing to come back the very next day and do it all again under the same or worse conditions.

109

I participated in many sit-ins. I'm not nor have I ever been a violent person, but I know what it means to fight for what you believe in. I believe in standing firm and not wavering in the face of adversity, but one thing is certain, I love me and I would never allow harm to come to me. I was put to the test during the sit-ins at the lunch counter at Woolworth's.

Across the South, a number of large chain stores, small five and dimes drug stores, and department stores had lunch counters. Shoppers would come into the stores when the doors first opened and with any luck for the stores they would stay there buying wares and would spend part of their afternoons dining with friends. The lunch counters or full restaurants became gathering places for politicians, religious leaders, and just friends, as long as you were white.

We had all known of the rules preventing Negroes from eating at Woolworth's and long after laws were passed preventing discrimination, this was in full practice. Students from Philander Smith had gone there, knowing they would be turned away. Like clockwork, as soon as they entered, they were told to leave or be arrested.

I decided it was time to face this injustice and work to make things right. For several days, we walked into that very lunch room at the busiest time of day and we took up seats at the counter. We were told to leave – but we stayed put. At first it started with just a few, but soon our numbers grew. It was spring of 1960 and the vile memories of the Central High School crisis were still on everyone's mind. I sat near the end of the counter and a man came by and on the first day of the protest this man poured a cup full of ice down my back. I wiped it off and continued to sit there.

The next day this same man entered the room and walked right toward me. I wondered what he planned this time. It didn't take long for me to find out. He poured a cup of hot coffee on my clothes. It burned, but I continued to sit there, my skin stinging, my clothes wet. I sat there.

On the third day, I experienced the greatest humiliation of all. This same man walked right toward me and looked directly into my eyes and without hesitation he spat tobacco juice in my face. I had endured all that I could. I had to hold my temper in check. I had to summon up the courage to remain calm and not resort to violence.

For the past four days, I had endured name calling and threats. We had been called horrible names but would not give in. With each passing day, we had pushed the protest to the limit.

On the fourth day as this same man approached, I stood and looked him in the eye.

"You have poured ice on me, hot coffee and you spat tobacco juice in my face. I am afraid you have mistaken me for Dr. King."

"What are you talking about?" he said.

Again I repeated, "You have mistaken me for Dr. King."

"How have I mistaken you for that man?"

"You see, Dr. King is nonviolent! You have been tormenting an ex-marine. If you spit on me one more time, you will not see a nonviolent soldier like Dr. King, you will see a United States fighting marine come out of me and trust me, you don't want to experience that!"

I stood and I walked out. When I returned the next day, he was there, but he dare not even look my way.

The numbers of protesters had grown in numbers so that the police eventually came to clear the crowd. Woolworth's management closed the counter and five Philander Smith students were arrested and charged with loitering and with creating a disturbance in a public place. When the chief of police arrived at the store, he found the students sitting quietly reading books and magazines.

A number of lawsuits were filed against stores in and around Little Rock. Several of the cases went as far as the U.S. Supreme Court. The argument was that in a number of the cases where people were arrested, including the Woolworth's, local criminal laws were used to help private business owners deprive customers of equal treatment. (National Park Service, Little Rock National Historic Site).

The sit-ins at the lunch counters were but just a sample of the protests that occurred and the injustices heaped upon us during this sometimes violent season of transition.

We negotiated for about a week for local businesses to desegregate. We talked with restaurant owners and movie houses. We developed a plan to bring the city of Little Rock into compliance with federal law. Some of the business owners wanted to wait. They said they wanted to wait until next week or next month. I would respond, "I don't have the right to tell my people that they could not exercise their rights until next week or next month." At every turn it seemed that white business owners were trying to delay the inevitable. They truly believed blacks were second-, third-, or fourth-class citizens, if there were such a thing. It would be just fine with them if things would just stay the way they were. They could run their businesses and satisfy their white customers and then simply sell a few things to the blacks to keep them happy and keep them out of sight as much as possible. However, some business owners identified with our plight. They were not bad people. They truly wanted to move ahead and put this chapter of American history behind them. They wanted to treat everyone as a customer and not a class or race. These good-hearted people were actually trapped, surrounded by forces over which they had no true control. They were taking orders from a number of groups, the biggest of which were store owners. Some of the national chain operators were dictating to their local store managers how they would conduct business. It was easy for them because they were not on the scene facing the daily protests, the demands from their loyal white customers. They faced the harsh reality of a justice system that had created a law which was difficult to enforce.

I suggested we could develop a plan to accomplish our goals in a week by desegregating in categories. For example on Monday, the movie houses would open their doors and on Tuesday the restaurants, and so on and so on.

Eventually it worked out – but it was anything but a smooth transition.

A Respite For The
March Of The Century

Amid our efforts to desegregate the lunch counters, there came word of a great march – a rally for freedom. It would be unlike any other demonstration in the history of this country. The great leader, Dr. Martin Luther King Jr., was calling on people – everyday working people to join him in a visible act that could send a message around the world. This event emulated a planned march on Washington in 1941. At that time, A. Philip Randolph organized a march on Washington to pressure President Roosevelt to guarantee jobs for black men and women during the war. The march had gained strength and attention, but was cancelled when the president acquiesced and made good on the demand. It was Randolph again who suggested the 1963 march. He and Bayard Rustin – a well known civil rights activist –discussed the possibility of making this a reality. King was on the same track and had received offers of support from actors Marlon Brando and Paul Newman. It was universally agreed that a massive show of force would be the only way to break the back of Jim Crow. This would send a message to the heart of the federal government and directly to the desk of the president. The leaders of the key organizations convened in New York. They were Roy Wilkins from the NAACP, James Farmer from C.O.R.E., John Lewis from SNCC, Whitney Young from the National Urban League, and of course, Dr. King representing the Southern Christian Leadership Coalition or simply the SCLC. Bayard Rustin and Randolph led the discussion and the plans were made.

This though would be different. We were to join thousands of people as we marched on the nation's Capitol. President John F. Kennedy asked the groups to cancel the march, feeling that this would just be a show and would not produce lasting results. The organizers were not to be deterred. It forced the president to embrace the movement even more and offer vocal support for the march

I had to be there. I had to see this for myself. I believed it would be one thing to be on the front lines of a battle in your own world. But it would be another to see the faces of people just like me in great numbers who too endured the struggle. I had seen big demonstrations, but certainly nothing like what I would experience in the shadows of the Lincoln Memorial. I took a bus from Little Rock to Washington, D.C. There were thousands of buses on the same route. All roads led to D.C. All over the country, it was hot. The temperatures were oppressive, but the spirits were high. Seeing the faces of the people who had walked and drove and rode planes and trains and automobiles gave us a sense of strength and power and reckoning like we had never experienced before. The signs called for equality and bore simple yet searing messages – the most poignant of which was four simple words, "I am a man!"

I would have no key role in this event – except to say, "I was there!" But that alone was enough for me. I was there. I would be there for a moment in history that would inevitably be replayed every single year – sometimes several times a year in the minds of those who were there and those who wish they had been alive at that time. With every single step toward the Lincoln Memorial, the masses grew larger. We were travel-wearied, yet strong-spirited, we had work to do. There was a vision of hope to be shared for the day when we were in total control of our lives – a time when the promises of the United States Constitution and the Bill of Rights would mean more than mere words. People were wilting all around me in the 90-plus degree heat. They were fainting for a moment, but they were on their feet again to complete their journey. This was a small price to pay for the value of a gathering that would be realized for generations to come. They raised their sanctified voices in songs and chants creating melodies of a brighter day. They were strong, resolute and clear in their message. They anxiously anticipated the main speaker of the day. Many speeches by others were given. Three-hundred thousand of us stood hanging on to every word. We were all courteous to each other, friendly though we had never met, unified though we had but one common interest. We were brothers and sisters who came from different parentage.

We sang – "We shall overcome – We shall overcome – some day!" I felt the words squeeze a tear from my eye as it streamed down my face and mixed with the beads of sweat that already dominated my body. Up until this point, I was just filled with excitement and the notion that at last there was hope against the Selmas, the Birminghams and the Montgomerys. It was a hope as James Weldon Johnson put it – an unborn hope that had died – but yet – with a steady beat – have not our weary feet come to the place for which our fathers sighed? We have come over a way that with tears has been watered. We have come – treading a path through the blood of the slaughtered. But not today – this was our hope. This was our salvation – and then Dr. King stood to speak.

"I am happy to join with you today in what will go down in history as the greatest demonstration for freedom in the history of our nation..."

I was a part of a great piece of American history.

I was working on conducting a voter registration drive, and I needed materials that could only be obtained by going to the state Capitol building. I needed maps and current registration rolls. I became hungry while, so I took a break to get some lunch. I truly had the foolish notion that since the Civil Rights Act had been passed, I could eat anywhere I wanted. The Capitol building had a fine cafeteria. In fact, I knew some of the people who worked there, so I went downstairs, grabbed a tray and some silverware and began to proceed down the line to select items from the display. I was looking at the salads when the woman who ran the eatery came up to me and said in a strong clear voice, "I am sorry sir, we don't serve Negras here!"

Without hesitation I said, "That's all right lady, I don't eat them either, so you don't need to serve me any negras . You need to serve me some roast beef!"

"What I mean is that you can't eat in here!" she said.

I began to start my lecture. "Did you know that the Civil Rights Act had been passed and signed by Lyndon Johnson on July 2, 1964?" I continued to recite to her the tenants of the law and her obligation to adhere to it. In short, she needed to serve me whatever I chose to eat and I would enjoy my meal at any table I chose in the cafeteria of the state capital building.

She listened, but then retorted, "I know all of this, but we are not going to comply until such time that the Supreme Court rules on its validity."

I said, "Madam, if you know the history I know, the act is in effect now. You don't have to wait on the Supreme Court. If you want to file a complaint or a brief with the Supreme Court, you are free to do that, but The Civil Rights Act is applicable now.

Before I was able to utter another word, two plain-clothes Arkansas State Police officers rose to their feet and told me, "The lady said you cannot eat in here, why don't your leave?"

"Well who are you?" I queried.

"Well that is not important, who we are. The important thing is that you leave."

"Well, you cannot tell me to leave unless you have authority to tell me to leave!"

They picked me up, one on each side. They suspended me in the air with firm grips on my arms and my legs. They carried me to the door and began to swing me back and forth. When they got a good motion, they tossed me into the air like a piece of garbage and waited for gravity to pull me to the hard surface of the Capital sidewalk. I landed in a crumpled heap, bruised, embarrassed, but most of all mad. For as I looked down at my legs, I realized I only had two suits of clothes in life and now the pants to one was ripped at the knee. These two troopers are charged with the responsibility of enforcing the law, instead they treated me like garbage and tossed me out, simply because I wanted something to eat. I was humiliated as I laid there. No one came to my aid. Instead, people laughed, others sneered, and yet more simply walked by as if nothing at all had happened. They had seen before, so for them this was nothing more than a common occurrence. I often wondered what they were really thinking – perhaps, "Will they ever learn?"

Fortunately, other people became aware of my incident, including a local news reporter who I had worked with years earlier. He latched onto the incident and created a story and saw it through. This reporter's story led to an upcoming event.

Religious leaders from around the South were appalled at what happened to me. They were so angered they organized a sit-in at the state Capitol building. These were no ordinary preachers. They were bishops and part of the hierarchy of the religious world throughout the south. They included four bishops from the Episcopal, Christian Methodist Episcopal, Catholic, and African Methodist Episcopal churches. They were joined by about 30 ministers. They gathered at the state house, locked arms, sang, prayed and then walked inside the building to sit in the cafeteria. It was widely reported in newspapers, radio and television. Once again, the heightened sensitivity of negative coverage of racial incidents in Little Rock forced change.

The U.S. Attorney received an injunction forcing the cafeteria management to serve anyone who came there to dine. The cafeteria acquiesced and soon thereafter people of all colors were able to eat like whites at this once segregated cafeteria.

This is exactly what John F. Kennedy spoke about. People should not be forced to protest or become subject to violent acts for the mere pleasure of enjoying the rights and privileges of being an American. I was a former U.S. Marine who was sent off to war at the demand of my country only to return to unfair treatment. If a bump and bruise and torn pants was what it took to bring about change, then sign me up.

"A Marine is a mighty man
He don't give a damn
A Marine is a mighty man
He'll fight and he don't give a damn!"

It came as no surprise to me that in many ways the faces of this struggle were the same faces I saw at war. We did not discuss it, but former black fighters for the country, defenders of freedom in uniform, assumed leadership roles in the Civil Rights Movement. We returned home war heroes, but we could not gain the dignity from those who we risked our lives to protect. We were determined to fight even here against an enemy we knew all too well. We knew the faces of oppression maintained a personal vow to expose and debase their cause, just as they had us.

After enduring the segregation by the marines, I decided I was going to enjoy the freedoms for which I had just fought. Men and women in the military decided not to take it anymore push for change. That was when Robert Whitfield filed suit against the residential housing department at the University of Arkansas. Also, Hamilton Holmes, Sr. and Charlene Hunter-Gault sought to enter the University of Georgia. In addition, Vivian Malone Jones and James Hood fought to enter the University of Alabama. This marked the beginning of a new era. They became a new breed of fighters who were not content with mere lawsuits to gain their rights. They were people committed to personal sacrifice. They were willing to step into the fray and offer themselves as the prototypes for change.

I worked for change all over Arkansas and sometimes into surrounding states. I would go wherever needed. The majority of my time was spent dealing with voter registration.

I once traveled to my home county, Lincoln County, near Gould. My birthplace always held a special place in my heart although there were tough times there – times I would just as soon forget. But then I remember those challenging times were placed in my life for a reason, a purpose. The lessons learned from difficulty are not soon forgotten. In my memory, they shall remain lest I travel that way again.

I was there because two young men had been arrested and jailed in Star City. The charge was they didn't have a light over the license plate on the back of their car. The arrest came at noon on a day in the month of July. I wondered how a police officer would know they didn't have a light over their license plate in the middle of the day in bright sunlight. This was clearly a false charge. What was the real reason they were jailed? It was because they were in the county conducting voter registration. White law enforcement officers were told strangers from out of town – outsiders –were "stirring up trouble." That was a common phrase, "outsiders stirring up trouble." Police officers knew why the men were there. They were not violent people; they did not come there to do harm, steal or swindle. They were there to inform those who didn't know that their vote was important. They had a right to be a part of a political process that would in time determine their future and the future of their children. The basic right had been denied through deception and it was to be made right. These two men were simply helping them to fill out the forms so that they could be included on voting rolls.

I arrived properly attired in a suit and tie. I always wore a shirt and tie and suit. I made a statement to the prying eyes who watched my every move once I hit the town limits. Strangers were easy to spot, especially if they were black and well-dressed. The only black people who wore a shirt and tie were a preacher or a doctor – and so assumed the attendant at the local filling station. As I was putting gasoline into my car, the attendant said to me, "Hot today, isn't it preacher?"

I replied, "Yes it is quite hot today."

All along the attendant was looking into my car and eyeballing my suit jacket lying on the back seat.

"What do you do, because you are not from here? You are a preacher aren't you?"

"No sir, I am not a preacher."

"Are you a teacher?"

"No sir, I am not a teacher."

"Are you a doctor?"

"No sir, I am not a doctor."

He said, "So what are you doing? I can tell you don't come from here!"

I said, "Sir, I am conducting a statewide voter registration campaign."

Well that registered with him because, of course, that is the reason those two young people were in jail.

"Well, then you must know the two radicals we have in jail down here. We don't like outsiders coming in here to stir up trouble."

I paused for a moment and let the southern drawl of this white man drip into my mind just like the bead of sweat that trickled down my brow. I took my time during that few seconds to come up with an appropriate response.

"Sir, if you want to call me an outsider, that won't fit. If you want to call me radical, and if you think voter registration is radical - then I am radical. I am not however, an outsider."

"What do you mean you are not an outsider?"

"I was born right over there in Gould, Arkansas which is fifteen miles from here. Do you know where Gould is?"

He said, "Yes, I know where it is."

"Well, I was born over there in Gould on Mr. Holthoff's plantation. Do you know who Mr. Holthoff is?"

He said, "Mr. Holtoff owns half of this county."

I know, I was born on his plantation." I said, "Across the street over there was where the county fair was always held. I won first place for a slop-fed hog when I was a 4-H Club boy. Do you know what the 4-H Club is?"

"Yes, I know what it is." This man was now visibly irritated and somewhat embarrassed.

"So you can call me what you want to call me, but you can't call me an outsider, I was born in this county. But if you want to say I am radical and you believe that voter registration is radical, then I am radical."

His lips were pursed and he didn't say anything more to me.

I paid for my gas and I left there and went to the jail to check on these two voter registration workers.

When I got there, I asked the sheriff to come out so that I might talk with him. The deputy behind the desk reluctantly got him. I began by telling the Sheriff who I was and the reason for my visit. I explained to him the charges against these two men were ridiculous and that they were simply doing what they were entitled to do. I further explained that if they were not freed, there would be a massive demonstration in his small town and then everyone would know of this injustice and word would spread very rapidly and he would be embarrassed by the outcome. I must have struck a nerve, because a few minutes later both men were freed and nothing more was said about the charges. I didn't know for sure that my presence there would work, but it did and I am grateful that the men were unharmed while in custody. The two men left with me and we continued our work.

The voter registration was so important. If we could secure an individual's registration, we would ensure their fair participation in elections and allow them to escape from the poll tax levied in some counties. This was crucial because on some large farms or large places of employment, the business or farm owners would pay the poll tax for his workers. He then would use the poll tickets and cast votes on their behalf denying them a chance to vote for whomever they chose. Although the tax was only a dollar or two, it was discriminatory and was a precondition of the exercise of the right to vote. The poll tax was developed in the mid 19th to 20th century. After blacks were granted the right to vote, the poll tax was enacted as a means of preventing people from participating in the process. This was particularly harmful to Negroes and Native Americans, as well as poor whites who immigrated to the areas. Many times the poll tax included a "grandfather clause." That meant that any adult male whose father or grandfather had voted in a specific year prior to the abolition of slavery could vote without paying the tax. The tax was eventually outlawed in 1964 as part of the 24th Amendment.

To our benefit, we were able to conduct our work and leave unmolested by the law or vigilantes. I would not be so fortunate on other occasions.

The call for equality came much slower in the rural areas, outside the cities where people were not under the close scrutiny and watchful eyes of the courts. Rural blacks were greatly outnumbered and their voices fell on deaf ears. They would rely on the help of the organizations and the large numbers of people of color from the cities. Until they received assistance, they were on their own, powerless, helpless and at the mercy of the majority. People were fiercely independent and could care less what a court hundreds of miles away had mandated. Whites had been in power here so long they knew nothing else and change came slow or not at all.

I would drive hundreds of miles – all alone. I was left to my devices, my own skills, my own wit and wisdom to propel me through the darkness and to the next stop where my work was needed. I would face danger, for the people I would encounter were not always sympathetic or supportive of my cause. I would be in solitude many nights with my thoughts, questions and my mind that sometimes raced from one scenario to another. I would remember the dangers of the mobs at Central High School in Little Rock. I would replay those scenes over and over again. I would summon up those memories from the farms where I worked and the faces I would see, and the people, who through their actions commanded me to always press forward no matter what. I would recall the threats black people had faced – the burning crosses – the Ku Klux Klan raiding homes and attacking people who looked just like me. Fear and intimidation would keep these people from the polls or away from the schools. The threat of losing their jobs provided by the white majority would also hamper their efforts.

My mind would then focus on the smiling faces of my little girls, surrounding the love of my life and the mother of my children. I may have thought about quitting at some point had I allowed horrible memories to overrule my sense. Instead I channeled my thoughts on why I was there. I remembered my children and the children in my neighborhood and in my church and in my state and I would know immediately that I was there working for them – for their future. There was no room for fear; this was no place for hesitation. The cause was just and right and as it should be. There would have to be those like me who would sacrifice and who would be willing to give it their all. I liken my mission to a scripture that has been a testament for me and speaks to the need for service by us all. It beckons us to exhibit our selflessness for the good of others no matter the cost. It reminds us we answer to a greater command; to be of service to the least of these.

It makes us responsible for being the eyes and ears of those whose sight had been blocked and who were deafened by the cries of the helpless; the voiceless.

> *"I have shown you O man what doth the Lord require of thee but do justly, love mercy and walk humbly with thy God."*
> – Micah 6:8

"...walk humbly with thy God..." I know he is here with me – no matter where I go. He has guided my steps and directed my way and I shall show no fear. I may be frightened at times, and I may want to turn and flee, but I shall not. I trusted God to prepare me for the days ahead and allow me to accept the responsibility to do justly, love mercy and walk humbly. I am prepared for whatever shall come.

The history books have rightfully recorded the movements and the actions of Dr. Martin Luther King, Jr. He was the visible savior for Negroes, a voice and face people recognized and identified with the movement. He earned his place in history for what he did and what was done to him. I am telling these stories because there are so many more chapters of our history that have never been written. There are people, tens of thousands of them, who have never been identified, but who played important roles in the history of our nation. I weep for them and honor their sacrifice, no matter how small. I have seen some of their faces and I know what was done for me by those nameless and faceless heroes; they exist and I thank them, for me and for this nation. For without them, there may not have been an Ozell Sutton or there may not have been a you – who now reads these words and reflects with me on our journey and our story – a story that will never fully be told.

As time went by, I would find myself more and more on the road, driving from one city to the next, running voter registration programs and working to keep our workers out of trouble. Many more people would be stopped by local police and harassed simply for being where they were. Along the way, I made many friends who were sympathetic to our cause. These friends were of all colors, creeds, and races. Not all of them would be vocal in their support, but they would do their share of keeping us informed of progress and problems. It was a particular joy for me to run across people I knew, some as far back as the days of chopping cotton and living on the plantations. Some of these good souls would help. Others would find ways to support, but never showed their faces and never allowed their voices to be heard.

I experienced an example of the goodness and kindness of people of all races.

A fellow NAACP member and I were on our way home from a Youth Conference. The weather was bad, raining almost horizontally. It was blinding. We were on a rural road near Glasgow, Kentucky and a car passed us and we ran right off into a field. The car was broken and we were a long way from home. The accident happened a couple hundred yards from a house. The owner happened to see us and came to see what happened. I was naturally concerned because this was an area where people had been harmed in the past, just for passing through. As the farmer approached, he looked at us carefully and to my surprise, the first thing he said was, "Are you all right?"

We responded, "Yes, we are fine, but our car has been damaged."

"Well, there is a service station not far from here but it is not open now and there is nothing that you can do. I tell you what; my house is right over there. Come on and get into my truck and I will take you there and you can stay there for the night."

I was skeptical about this stranger, offering help to two black men on a dark and muddy road. However, there was little we could do at the moment, so we went along. When we arrived at his house, his wife was there and was preparing to bed down for the night. She made us some sandwiches and pointed us to a bedroom and we went to sleep. I was still wondering whether this was really happening. I did not know what made these people extend such kindness and hospitality to two perfect strangers.

We rose the next morning and went into the kitchen where the woman had made tea and biscuits for us. We sat at their kitchen table, ate the meal, thanked them and proceeded to leave the house. The man put us into his truck, got the tow truck and stayed with us until the car was ready. He bid us well, never really knowing the magnitude of his kindness or the people he was helping. As Dr. Martin Luther King Jr. may have put it, these were truly people of goodwill, whose voices had not been heard, whose course was unclear, and whose courageous acts had not been seen. They were representative of a good number of people in the South who were God-fearing, kind-hearted Christians who helped to bring about change.

I did not remember their names, but I remember their faces, and I shall never forget the lesson they taught me. Sometimes words fall short of expressing a person's intent and heart, it takes action and living by example, to be an example.

King had his entourage, and I had my foot soldiers, volunteers mostly who worked tirelessly for voter registration across the south. This effort gained more prominence in 1964 when a young lawyer from Washington moved to the south to head the Southern Regional Council's Voter Education Project. Tall, dark-skinned and bearing an eloquent voice, Vernon Jordan brought a new life and a new face to the effort I had been making throughout Arkansas. He would do exactly what I had been doing for some time, finding volunteers who would be willing to travel throughout the South and register voters. He would have to use his charm and training to encourage wealthy southerners to fund this effort. Before this time, we had been operating on a shoe-string budget and sometimes at the goodness and mercy of those who were sympathetic to our cause. Vernon Jordan was well-known throughout the country. I was well-known throughout Arkansas. I was glad that more attention was being given to this grassroots civil rights movement. I welcomed the help of anyone who could further educate our people who had been denied the simple constitutional rights guaranteed in a true democracy.

THE DEPARTMENT OF JUSTICE
COMMUNITY RELATIONS SERVICE

In 1966, I had been doing some consulting for the U.S. Commission on Civil Rights and had briefed them on what the Civil Rights Act contained. The White House convened a meeting to talk about civil rights. I made some contacts while there that led to a call that would change my life. This was my chance to work on the bigger stage of this movement. I received a telephone call from someone I met at the conference who was hiring for the Department of Justice. There was an opening for a field representative in the DOJ Office of Community Relations.

This division of the justice department was created with the signing of the Civil Rights Act of 1964. The federal government realized it had a responsibility to keep the calm in times of conflict and, if possible, avoid all conflict. The problem was they had no textbook strategy for resolving crises. This agency was dispatched to assist local governments, private and public organizations and community groups. Its mission was to resolve racial and ethnic tensions, incidents and civil disorders, restore racial stability and harmony. (From CRS DOJ)

The members of the Community Relations Service team were many times invisible. We avoided media attention and focused our energies on the people who were directly involved or on those who had the power and ability to prevent disorder. Moreover, we always remain neutral, not taking sides, but getting as close to the people at the core of the problem as possible. This required me to enter a problem spot with an open mind. We were there to protect the rights of everyone involved. We didn't have to like or dislike the people we were working with, we were just there to listen, and act. I would talk as easily with the Grand Dragon of the Ku Klux Klan as I did with the president of the NAACP. Regardless of their views, these were American citizens who enjoyed all the rights and privileges of the Constitution, the Bill of Rights, and the Declaration of Independence. My love of people and Lula Belle's teachings had prepared me for this job and the tasks that lie ahead.

JACKSONVILLE, FLORIDA

The first few days of my job with the Justice Department were consumed with getting to know what the agency did in terms of conflict resolution. Never before in the history of the country had a federal agency been charged with such an awesome responsibility. We were the sole branch of the United States government that worked exclusively on a grassroots level to pre-empt violence and other forms of conflict. There was no shortage of cases. This was a turbulent time in the history of our country. Most every state in the country had some pockets of resistance when it came to the equal treatment of all citizens. The federal laws were damned in the minds of those who chose to cleave to the history of oppression that was so pervasive for centuries. There are those who would rather die and be buried before they would sit at the table with someone of another race or ethnic background. This made the existence of the Community Relations Service that much more viable and valuable.

We were still a relatively small agency forced to deal with big problems. After being in the department for four days, I was told to get on a plane and head to Jacksonville, Florida.

I knew very little about the conflict in Jacksonville except the fact that there had been some rioting in the city. I didn't even have credentials. All I had was a letter of introduction. So with this piece of paper, I was about to dive right into a case that could have ended very badly were it not for cooler heads prevailing. Before my arrival, the Jacksonville Police Department had little success in keeping the peace.

Jacksonville had been a city on the verge of turmoil for a number of years, and like most southern cities the central point of contention was the integration of schools.

In Jacksonville, there were two high schools less than half a mile from each other. Ribault High School was all white and Raines High School was all black. City leaders had some success in getting black students to integrate Ribault High. The same could not be said for Raines High. Whites refused to attend the all-black school. In fact, when black students went to Ribault, some white parents began taking their children out and thus the so-called "white flight" began to take wings.

Tensions between black and white students continued to build for some time until one afternoon a fight broke out between a white student and a black student. It started as a disagreement between two people and grew into a near race riot. For several days, the unrest continued and spilled over into the neighborhoods. At one point the schools were closed in an effort to cool tempers.

Jacksonville was no stranger to this type of violence. The city had experienced previous confrontations. It had been an historic clash on June 25, 1964 at a "Whites only" section of beach in St. Augustine, Florida. Dr. King had been there. He went to observe and to meet with the local NAACP over the issues they faced. While staying in a rented beach cottage, someone fired a shot through the glass door. Dr. King was arrested days later while trying to be served in a segregated restaurant. Civil rights groups had secured a meeting with the white officials, but limited progress had been made. Whites remained reluctant to participate and support the cornerstone of equal treatment. This was a time of tension and turmoil that would last as long as all the sides involved refused to talk and more importantly refused to listen.

The city had witnessed this one small incident escalate into near chaos. There was nothing like looking into the eyes of human rage. It could not be fully described. I had seen it over the years and I would see it on my first assignment with the Department of Justice. There were areas in the black community where fires had been set, cars overturned, and rocks and bottles thrown, mostly at the police. The violence was contained to a small area, but there was the fear it would grow to other neighborhoods. That is what frightened city leaders the most. God forbid it spilled into the white neighborhoods or their businesses. That would have resulted in an all-out war.

I had been with the agency long enough to learn how to use a government voucher to purchase a plane ticket. I boarded a plane and arrived midday in Jacksonville. After presenting credentials and another voucher, I secured a car – no radio, the radio was extra and it was a "luxury" that my agency would not fund. I had no map, so I had to ask people where to go, how to find the local police station and city hall. The down side to that was that people knew immediately you were not a local and some people always feared the agitation of outsiders. I eventually found what I was looking for. I met separately with the police, city leaders, black leaders and youth leaders. After meeting separately, I asked a representative of all the parties involved to join me at city hall.

Jacksonville's issues were so numerous. The city was wrestling with integration and the consolidation of the city and county governments. The timing was right for these problems to come to an end. City leaders knew they would need the support of the black community. Also, Blacks knew this and used this as a major bargaining chip. The effort was to develop a method of coexistence that satisfied everyone, at least for the time being. I was delighted all interested parties involved were actually anxious to talk although everyone had a large agenda and not all problems could be solved with this one initial gathering. This allowed me to help bring everyone together – and to back out – letting them solve their own problems. The violence came to an end. The tension remained. My work was done – for now – as long as the peace would hold.

In the years to come, they reached agreements to open parts of the city to blacks, including parks, recreation facilities and other public spaces. There also was a guarantee for representation by blacks on the city council. Three black districts were created. Parks near black communities were improved. Streets were paved and city services were increased. I was proud to have assisted with these improvements, but I could not take credit for doing so. I arrived in Jacksonville at a time when the parties were actually ready to talk, but they didn't know how. It took another crisis to open the doors of communication and to bring about change. If only all my cases would work out this way.

SHREVEPORT, LOUISIANA

My second assignment was in Shreveport, Louisiana. This southern city rests almost smack dab in the middle of Dallas, Little Rock, New Orleans and Houston. I had been informed that Blacks were being denied an opportunity to eat at local restaurants. I went there to investigate. I decided to visit one of the most popular eateries. It was located inside a drug store. There was a large counter toward the back of the store. The traditional bar stools were in front of the counter and a few booths further back. The cooking area was clearly visible from the counter. I chose a seat at the counter and prepared to order a meal. A hostess came by, and I said, "One for lunch."

She scowled at me and said "I'm sorry, but we don't serve Negroes here."

"What do you mean you don't serve Negroes here? Don't you know about the Civil Rights Act?"

She cut me short and said "Yes, I know about it, but we will not comply until it is enacted by the state. You will have to leave!"

I knew it would be a futile attempt, but I needed to try one more time to convince this business of its error in thinking and its illegal action.

I planted my feet and glared back at the woman, "Don't you know that this is a federal law? It does not have to be approved by the state for it to be an enforceable law!"

Again she asked me to leave. I did so, knowing full well what had transpired and what had to happen next.

I knew right then that there would be no need for a sit-in here. This was something we could solve very quickly. I found a local agency that was similar to the Arkansas Council on Human Relations and talked with its leadership. They became excited about this issue especially since there was now a federal official here who had the power to bring more attention to a problem they had been living with for some time. There was a young man who was the deputy director of the local NAACP office. His name was Leon Tarver, in the years to come he would become the president of Southern University in Baton Rouge, Louisiana.

We decided to go back to the restaurant with both black and white "patrons". The white patrons were seated with no problem at all. The black patrons were told to leave. This was our proof. This is what we needed, a clear documentation of the actions of the restaurant which was clearly a violation of federal law. With this information we contacted a local federal judge and without delay we received notice that an injunction was filed against the Northern Louisiana Restaurant Association. The courts contacted the restaurants and informed them that they were enjoined from discriminating.

For most of the areas of the country where discrimination existed, business owners knew their days were numbered. However, they held to their beliefs and their practices until they were challenged; until they were caught. This means that if no one called their actions into question; if no one was there to seek legal remedies, then the practice would continue. In some cases, this happened for years after the federal laws were passed. If it had not been for the work of many dedicated people known and unknown, the laws of the land would not be enforced. In some areas, blacks had been so intimidated they would shudder at the thought of raising their voices in opposition to the atrocities.

For many years after that first visit to Shreveport, I would keep in contact with the people. I found it important to maintain a connection and to let them know where I was and how long I would be there. They were my eyes and ears and they would keep me informed of progress and problems in their area.

NEW ORLEANS
DESEGREGATING THE FRENCH QUARTER

The mere mention of New Orleans and its residents automatically conjures thoughts of its most famous slogan, "Laissez Les Bon Temps Roulez" or "Let the Good Times Roll." Those thoughts were coupled with Cajun-seasoned food, scrolled wrought iron balconies in The French Quarter, and Mardi Gras. These are all pleasant thoughts that capture the essence of the city of good times. New Orleans has always been thought of as melting pot of cultures and ethnicities. But this city was enduring some of the same racial injustices as other southern cities. One of my cases involved being dispatched to the Crescent City to investigate claims that restaurants and bars in the French Quarter were not allowing Blacks to eat and drink. I knew from past experiences that if the complaints existed, then in reality it was true. I knew, too, that in order to bring about change, those in charge had to be confronted with facts stating the problem and in the best of worlds they would also respond to a reasonable plan for change. My plan was the same as it was in other cities. I would go down to the restaurants with six people, a bi-racial group. We would choose a restaurant at random and as a group ask to be seated. As soon as the maître'd would see the racial makeup of the group, the restaurant was suddenly "full" and would remain so for the foreseeable future. We would face the same treatment at each restaurant. Our next course of action would be to immediately send in a whites-only group. Consequently, the restaurant suddenly had available tables. I would document these incidents and then report back to my agency with details of the level of discrimination.

My supervisor at the time ordered me to meet with the mayor of New Orleans in an effort to avert an injunction and other possible problems. The sitting mayor at the time was Victor Schiro, an Italian-American who had lived in Honduras and California before moving back to New Orleans. Schiro was reared by his parents in New Orleans. Now as mayor, he was quite a character, having been a minor celebrity in his own right, including being an extra in movies, and later as a radio announcer in New Orleans. He had worked in the insurance business for a while before considering a life of public service. Schiro worked his way up the ranks in city government and had served as parks commissioner, council member and eventually mayor. However, this man of the people was a staunch segregationist.

I was still relatively new to the job, but now I was about to take on a leader of a city, a man who was revered by other politicians and his constituents. He had closed the public swimming pools rather than desegregate them. Schiro was practical and ushered in the integration of city schools without a major incident, thus protecting the city from the negative stereotypes of other southern cities that had major clashes in the streets. This protected the business climate of the city and also protected the mayor from ridicule. However, restaurants and bars were a different story.

I met with Mayor Schiro in his office at city hall. As I arrived at the ornate city hall building, I flashed my credentials indicating I was from the United States Department of Justice. I found that most of the time I didn't need to be so official, but this was clearly a case of Daniel going into the lion's den. This was a man who was used to getting his way. He was not very tall and displayed the strong dark features of his Italian heritage. A thick black moustache rested above his top lip and he was dressed in a dark well-fitted suit, white shirt and an impressive tie. A pocket square peeking out of his breast suit pocket spoke loud and clear that this was a man who liked to dress well. In stark contrast, I liked to dress well too, but did not have the funds to match this man's apparel. My clothes were more of the 'Government Issue' brand, plain loose fitting, but nevertheless the uniform of professional people working on a modest salary.

Mayor Schiro knew why I was there. He had made up his mind about what he was going to do. When I arrived he clearly saw I was a black man. I was just another black man with government credentials in the eyes of most white people in the South. I reviewed with him the information we had gathered in our preliminary investigation and told him he needed to work with the businesses to encourage them to comply with The Desegregation Act of 1964. He glared at me with disdain and was offended by my forthrightness in telling him to make things right. Few people told Victor Schiro what to do.

Schiro sat near me in a chair in his office, displaying a posture of superiority and he locked his eyes with mine and said, "How well do you think I know Lyndon Johnson? I can have your job before you reach that door."

I touched his knee and summoned up a slight smile, "I know you can get me fired – it's all a matter of whether you will or not. Let me also remind you that you have an application for a large sum of money from Housing and Urban Development to replenish the French Quarter. As long as there is segregation in the French Quarter you will not get a dime!"

Once again he used his connections to the president, "I can and will get you fired!"

Unraveled by the comment, I replied, "That's OK then. I will go back to my days of protest before coming to work for CRS. I will tie up the French Quarter with hundreds of people calling for a boycott. I will hold a press conference from the jail if I need to, and people will come from all over to assist in tying up business in the French Quarter. We will cause problems, and, as you know, whites are afraid to socialize and spend their money in a place where there are problems. There won't be any customers there. The restaurants and bars will be empty. The streets will be filled with protesters who won't spend money while the businesses remain empty!"

While there was no look of defeat in his eyes, there was the acknowledgment that perhaps working with the businesses to desegregate would, in the end, be better for the city. Victor Schiro, the consummate politician knew what was best for his city and without hesitation agreed to work with the businesses in this regard. I can't take credit for desegregating the French Quarter, but it was the first step that would lead to New Orleans becoming one of the most popular places to visit for African Americans. It was this act that brought millions of people to the city for conventions and major festivals and fairs. Each time I go there, I remember those days when I nor anyone who looked like me, could eat in the four-star restaurants. Since that time, I go there and enjoy myself like anyone else who has strolled along Canal Street. But in my mind, I remember that tough politician and the nervous young black man who met and brought about a change everyone can enjoy.

In the weeks and months to come, I would be dispatched to any number of hot spots in the South. I faced the same issue, but yet the situation was different. If we were called into action it was because the rights and privileges of someone were threatened. If we were on an airplane heading into a hot zone or in a car speeding down back country roads, there was the glimmer of hope that we could prevent violence or that violence had already occurred and we were one of the keys to a resolution. Each time I was given an assignment, I prayed my work would be successful. Deep down in my soul, I always wanted to be used as an instrument for peace. I have always hoped people could be caring and understanding of each other. That was my hope – a hope that was constantly slapped in the faced with the stark and stinging reality of this time in history that was ever so tumultuous. But unlike James Weldon Johnson's lyrics, I was bound and determined to let unborn hope have a chance at life. That could only happen if I continued to believe that I could make a difference and if I let my God use me as an instrument of his divine and everlasting peace. My risks would be worth it because the cause was too great. I knew lives were at stake, rights were at issue, and dignity needed to be preserved.

"Martin"

I cannot mention the Civil Rights Movement and not conjure up the image of a man who grew to symbolize this effort. The movement was trademarked around the world by the young face of a black man who grew up on Auburn Avenue near the heart of downtown Atlanta. The Reverend Dr. Martin Luther King, Jr. was always a powerful presence. The mere mention of his name would elevate the spirits of those who heard it, at least those who were ready for change. If his name was called, one could almost hear his voice. People were drawn to the man with that distinctive resonating voice laden with a sophisticated and educated Southern drawl. He was their Moses. He was their Harriet Tubman. He was their only hope.

However, some people labeled Dr. King as a rabble rouser, an instigator, an outsider who came to town to stir up trouble, to create havoc and then leave. Dr. King did not travel alone. He would always go to a town or city with backup – throngs of people who would travel miles to be in his presence or to be a part of his team. We became familiar with the faces that joined him in this movement. For instance, Andrew Young, a minister with a boyish face and gentle demeanor who later became a member of congress, was often an arm's length from Dr. King. Young would later become the U.S. Ambassador to the United Nations, mayor of Atlanta, Georgia, a businessman, consultant, philanthropist and much sought-after speaker.

Rev. Ralph David Abernathy was highly visible in the movement and was a protest leader for much of his college and adult life. Dr. Abernathy led demonstrations on his own college campus at Alabama State University in Montgomery, Alabama. He organized the yearlong bus boycott in Montgomery after Rosa Parks was arrested for refusing to give up her seat to a white man on a city bus. Abernathy would later become the second in command of the Southern Christian Leadership Conference.

Rev. Hosea Williams was another face seen many times with Dr. King. He was the son of two teenagers who were committed to an institution for the blind. His mother ran away when she learned she was pregnant. He never knew his father and was raised by his grandparents. He left their home at the age of 14. Hosea joined the army and was part of an all-black unit under General Patton. He was the only survivor of a Nazi bombing and spent months in the hospital. This man was a fighter. He had to be. His life was so frothed with confrontation, disappointment, mistreatment, and abandonment that fighting was his means of survival. This spirit would propel him into the heart of the Civil Rights Movement. He was hospitalized again after being beaten nearly to death for drinking from a "whites only" water fountain. Throughout his life, Hosea was arrested more than 125 times for his involvement in protests and demonstrations. He remained loyal to Dr. King and the people he came to represent, no matter the danger, cost, or what other people were saying and doing.

The youngest face in the crowd with Dr. King was a large man who wore an Afro. He usually donned jeans and a denim jacket. He was a graduate of North Carolina A&T in Greensboro, North Carolina, and he spoke more like a militant than all the rest of the Martin lieutenants. He was Jesse L. Jackson, born in Greenville, South Carolina. Like most of the people in King's inner circle; Jackson was a Baptist minister, though he never earned a degree in theology, he was ordained and later received honorary degrees. Jackson was recognized by Dr. King for his work in Chicago where he was instrumental in working to get white businesses and the local government to award contracts to black companies. He also worked in efforts to feed the hungry through the Southern Christian Leadership Conference's Operation Breadbasket. Jackson was quite the speaker and like Dr. King had the gift of raising the level of excitement at rallies and protests. Jackson was highly regaled as the voice of the young – a liaison of sorts to growing numbers of college-aged people who brought energy to the movement.

Many more people were part of King's inner circle. They were the soldiers who walked in the same steps as their leader – sometimes before him – other times behind him. They were always there. They showed the white establishment there was some organization to this movement and that there was a hierarchy and the strength of several layers of people who served as foot soldiers, planners and facilitators. Others oversaw logistics, procurement and of course fundraising.

Anywhere King would go, an entourage would already be there – planning and organizing in advance of his arrival. His time was precious, although he never appeared pressured by time. He exhibited the Southern gentile of talking to nearly anyone who would speak to him. He had a tremendous peripheral vision. He paid as much attention to people on either side of him and sometimes those hidden from view as he did to those who had big names, titles and degrees. King knew this was a mission for and by the least of these. These were God's children. This was God's calling. This was a God-driven ministry of sorts to convert souls to believe in racial equality.

It was a warm day in Memphis, Tennessee in April 1968. The noonday temperatures were starting to rapidly climb signaling the coming of another sweltering hot summer. Springtime is all about life – an awakening from the winter chill that lulled animals and plants alike to a gentle sleep and a slower pace. Spring is about a newness of life and a call to awaken. But somehow this seasonal rite of passage into spring was not visible. It was hidden by the cloud of the mounting racial tension. People protested throughout Memphis against the unfair treatment of the city's sanitation workers. Dr. King and his legions of followers were there. I was there along with a cadre of people from the Justice Department. Our office of community relations had several people there. This was a big series of events involving meetings and rallies and marches. This situation had been simmering since January.

When the sanitation workers started their protest, I was called by a Justice Department official George Pembleton. He said, "Ozell, we want you to get to Memphis."

I had read something about the conflict, and teasingly I said, "And do what?"

He said, "You're the one person I'm sparing who will know what to do once you're there. So just get there."

Before I left, I gathered information to assist me when I arrived. I had to assess the conflict, including identifying the involved parties.

I knew the sanitation workers were involved. I just needed to find out particularly who was leading the sanitation workers and where their leadership was based. I knew their concerns were with the city of Memphis, so I needed to find out what powers in the city were pulling the strings. I had to determine the role of the mayor and city council. I had to simply confer with people. I went to the leaders of the sanitation workers to find out their demands. They had circulated their information everywhere, anyway, in the newspaper and in community leaflets. I sat down with the parties to see where they stood on the issues. I was attempting to determine how to resolve the problem. Of course, each side was willing to tell you without hesitation. The sanitation workers contended they were very low paid and not being treated as human beings. They too wanted their dues write-offs.

Unions did not usually collect the money from the union members. Instead, the city, or whomever they were working for collected the money and they paid the union. Union dues write-off resulted in a withdrawal from their paycheck. The city refused to give a dues write-off because they refused to recognize the union. During these meetings it was easy for me to surmise that not only did the city disagree with the unionization of sanitation workers, they objected because the majority of the workers were black.

Union members had power as a result of the city's recognized union. The union had bargaining rights freely granted by the city. But the relationship with the city and the union changed. The city did not want to give up its power to control its workers and the amount they were paid, most especially to a group of black men. The union stepped up its protest, moving to more than just rioting and picketing. They moved to mass demonstrations.

The city chose to interfere with the demonstrations to simply give the marchers pure hell. That was the kind of climate that was going on by the time we got to Memphis in late February and March.

By this time, King, the union and the black leadership in Memphis joined the union in protest. The black ministers, the NAACP, and other civil rights organizations had sided with the union. Almost everywhere Dr. King ever went, he was invited in. He didn't particularly start the movement. When King went to Memphis, this further shed more light on the movement. They had big mass meetings every night with eight or ten thousand people. They had marches every Saturday. Dr. King lifted the protest to another level when we showed.

Amid their weekend meetings and protests, our role was to try to keep the situation peaceful by persuading the city not to do anything to further inflame the situation. Their protests were inflamed by police action, occurring out of ignorance and deliberately by others. For example, city officials insisted the marchers could only occupy one side of a street. The police insisted that if anybody stepped across the centerline, they would be arrested. They were sometimes arrested when they really didn't step across the line. The police harassed them about any little thing that they could come up with.

I had three people assigned to me from the Justice Department's community relations service. One was Jim Laue of George Mason University's conflict resolution program, and Fred Miller. We divided the chores. Jim, who was white, was assigned to SCLC. His job was to know at all times what they were going to do. He would try to persuade them not to do anything that inflamed the situation by getting them not to protest violently.

Jim was assigned to King. I was assigned to the police and the courts. Jim Laue knew King's coworkers well. He had done research for them and he had actually done consulting with them. So, he knew them very well. I knew them, but not in the same kind of detail that he did.

I was supposed to make sure police commanders and officers knew exactly who I was, why I was there and what I was trying to do. I was supposed to know at all times, as much as I could how the police were going to respond to everything. I reported to the commanders when I saw police officers out of line in those marches. I said, "They just simply harass the marchers all of the time, trying to provoke something out of innocence." That was my job. I was too a liaison with the court, talking to the judge about his orders, determining if they were effective in doing what he set out to do, or if the orders started more problems. In addition, I was the only person who could go to housing project workers, invade the group of young black militants, and talk with them. The others were reluctant to do that. Everybody else was scared to do it. But I come from the old school of thought which suggests, "Fools rush in, but angels dare to try". I've always found I could talk to the militants very, very well. I did so without any fear, because most of the fear about what's going to happen was in my head, not actual, and I knew that. I knew they weren't going to harm me. I wasn't their problem. I spoke with them and they just cut me off and said I was talking damn stupid. But that didn't bother me.

However, I was always concerned about groups of people who were referred to as "The Invaders." These were young people who were absolutely opposed to nonviolent techniques. They advocated violence, and they provoked it. They were of the belief that the passive nonviolent approach not only didn't work, but it took too long to bring about results. King's last march broke up in disarray, and it was believed to be the result of The Invaders breaking out windows. It was not the marchers who started the vandalism. We believed it was The Invaders, and their followers who did, which provoked the police to attack the marchers. The police fell right into their trap. Their plan all along was to attract violence. The seven or eight thousand marchers were doing nothing. The deputy chief of police was commanding the street. I always marched in that gray area between the marchers and where the press was taking pictures. I was always in that area, in front of the marchers between them and the cameras. The deputy police chief came up to me and said, "Mr. Sutton, we got to do something about this march, I may have to stop it." I said, "Chief, you can't stop this march, it stretches out for miles back there. If you stop the people in front, the others are going to keep coming; they don't even know the march is stopped in that sense. Then you've got chaos." And then he said, "Where is Dr. King?" I said, "Dr. King is over in that line, about three or four lines back. He usually started up front, but folk got in front of him in these marches. You'll find him." He said, "No, I'm not going in there. Would you go in there and tell Dr. King to come out?" So I went in there like a fool and got Dr. King to come out. And while I'm in there, all hell broke loose. Police officers started shooting tear gas, swinging billy club sticks, and used water hoses. Community relations officials quickly got Dr. King out of that situation. A car rolled up and they shoved Dr. King in the car and the car got out of there.

City police officers were anxious for the march to fail. The violence played right into the hands of the police. They feared there would be trouble, thanks to The Invaders.

When the violence erupted police officers began to drive the Blacks back toward the church. They were pushing, shoving and beating the people back. They had no choice but to move backwards or be beaten. About that time a police officer runs up to me with a long riot stick and he pokes me in the stomach with that stick and he told me to "get." There was a lot of noise – deafening loud noises. All I could do was holler at the officer. I knew I was within my rights, and so were the marchers. I would not run, and I couldn't fight. I couldn't fight because I didn't have anything to fight with. He had a stick and a gun. I had nothing. He began to wail on me with that stick repeatedly telling me, "Get." Now, if I'd have had some sense, I would have run or tried to identify myself as an employee of the Department of Justice. He wanted me to run. But I wouldn't do that. I stood there weaving and bobbing trying to avoid serious injury. He became angry because he couldn't hit my head. Even with my big head, I ducked it near the height of my shoulders. He beat up my shoulders and arms pretty good, but he never hit my head. I would later recount to others that if they thought Muhammad Ali could do a rope-a-dope, they should have seen me. I would have made Muhammad Ali look like a neophyte. I was able to avoid serious blows to the head, but a young white man, named Stansfield, played a vital role in saving me. I knew him from the days I was director of the Arkansas Council on Human Relations. When I was director of the Arkansas Council on Human Relations, he was director of the Virginia Council on Human Relations. I had gone on to work for community relations service and he'd come down to Memphis to work with the Southern Regional Council. He was a field rep for the Southern Regional Council. It seemed to be a small world. We all knew each other. Stansfield stepped down off the side-walk, grabbed me by my arm and stashed me up where he was.

The violence continued for some time. The militants who started the confrontation took the violence a step further. They looted stores and caused uncalled for damage to cars and businesses. I was terrified and in great pain. Even though the police officers knew I was with the Justice Department, they didn't care. When the confrontation started, the police officers pulled off their badges so their names couldn't be identified. When the ruckus was over, I went tearing down to the police department. I went to see the deputy police chief to tell him what happened to me.

I knew I would not be able to answer his questions. "Do you know who hit you?" he said.

I should have seen this coming. "Of course I don't know who hit me."

He said, "Well, if I knew who hit you I could deal with it, but there's nothing I can do."

I said, "Chief, you knew the men didn't have on badges or their nameplate, so how could I tell you who hit me?"

He said, "Well, all I can say is I'm sorry."

I had come to expect this type of treatment. It didn't matter that I was representing the government of the United States. The officer only saw was a black face – just one more black face that he could do without.

Later that evening when that march was broken up, they had the mass meeting just as they had on previous evenings. This one would be different though because the emotions were high and people were still stinging from the attack by the police. Once again, I had been looking directly into the face of human rage. This face was white and it wore a uniform. This was the image etched into the minds of those in attendance of this rally – an image they would not soon forget. The conversations that evening retold of how some people escaped without being hit, but were doused with fire hoses or had swallowed the acrid air clouded by tear gas. No one had done anything wrong – no one who had a serious interest and stake in this march. It was a small number of young men who had elevated a peaceful demonstration to a near riot. No matter what happened or who started it, this was the very fuel that signaled to the organizers that the marches must continue. Also, protestors asked the lingering question of whether the violence was in fact started by the young invaders. This group of young men had become well organized and while they did not agree with all the methods of Dr. King, they certainly knew they had to live in that city and they were subject to arrest like anyone else. Our suspicions were even more real after hearing a conversation with Charles Cabbage. He was one of the Invaders and widely thought to be the leader of the group. Cabbage had reported that on occasion some faces he did not recognize would show up. These were people who would show a keen interest in the planning of demonstrations and all the details which led them to believe they were possible government infiltrators.

Violence was just what the city would want to show that the people involved were a threat to their way of life. The daytime violence and looting of stores by a few played right into the hands of Mayor Henry Loeb III. In a news conference after the incident Loeb said:

> *"When the march which was to be permitted, had it remained orderly – that generated into a riot – abandoned by its leaders, the*

police with my full sanction took the necessary action to restore law and order and to protect the lives and property of the citizens of Memphis. The police are continuing and will continue to do so with the help of the sheriff of Shelby County, the governor's representative Claude Armour, the highway patrol and the National Guard units that are presently in the city."

King was in agreement with the notion that he could not give up the fight and he must return to Memphis. So he was scheduled to come back the following week. King wanted to truly demonstrate that he could lead a nonviolent march in Memphis.

King flew home to Atlanta. Before he could arrive, word of the violence had hit the streets and was all over the media. This was not what King had planned. It is not the way community relations services had envisioned this movement developing. There was wide criticism of King, and not just from whites. Some blacks were not in agreement with King and his methods. King was urged to abandon support of the sanitation workers. Consequently, he was faced with a mounting scrutiny from the Federal Bureau of Investigation. J. Edgar Hoover tried to discredit The Civil Rights Movement and especially tried to destroy King. People circulated rumors that some of the actions of local police and some of the demonstrators were orchestrated by forces in the federal government. But this would not deter King. He was going back. He was going to prove that these types of rallies and protests were not only useful and effective, but they were necessary.

King went back to Memphis. On April 3, 1968, there was a rally for the sanitation workers. King was going to be the featured speaker. He became upset because he worried that the turnout would be small. He asked his close friend Dr. Ralph Abernathy to speak in his place. He was afraid that if he spoke before a smaller crowd than the one he had on his previous trip, it would be played up in the media as a failure. King got a call at the hotel. An estimated two thousand people were there and he was urged to come to the rally.

Dr. King got there and delivered the last speech of his young life. Every time since that day when I hear the recording of it, I get chills. It sounded as if he was predicting his own death. The speech in time would be referred to as *"The Mountaintop Speech."* This speech was nothing short of eloquent delivered in true King fashion. It was laced with analogies and biblical references and historical facts. It chronicled some of the highlights of the movements. King made several comments that he was glad to have been blessed to see "this time" in the history of the nation.

This speech was to be like none other delivered by Dr. King. You have heard it before…the Mountaintop Speech. It would be different in content, in tone and in history in terms of its significance.

This was to be the last major speech given by the man anointed to be the leader of America's black people.

If you ever had a chance to look at the video from this speech you can look into Dr. King's eyes and tell that something was different. This was not a speech that had been fully written. King likely had a sketch of the text he had hoped to deliver, but like many great speakers, you must summon up the words based upon the audience and based upon what is happening in your life at that time. These words were prophetic. All throughout the marches and the rallies it was Dr. King who was the deliverer of the message of hope. Instead on this occasion he was more reflective and more resigned to a fate that had not yet come. I listened and I watched the crowd. They knew it too. They sensed the air of finality. It was the reference to the untimely end to life and the resolution that all is well.

In his text, Dr. King pointed out that those in power had ample opportunity to deliver on the promises of bringing black people out of the vestiges of inequality and unfair treatment based on race. He looked at the changes that had been made and were occurring under his watch. He also marveled at the fact that change had been made and that he was thankful that he had witnessed through his eyes some minor changes….changes that were not enough. More had to be done.

We all knew or at least had the sense that this Movement would have an ending of sorts or that there would be those things that held us back. The death of our leader was not in our sights – not now…not at the very moment that change was just around the corner – at least for these sanitation workers.

If you go back and look at Dr. King's speech – it was not just the words that ring clear… It is the cadence, the rhythm, the tone and the look. The look in his eyes told the story. Of course we had no idea what was too happen…but he did.

In the speech he made references to Moses – as he did on many occasions… He proffered the notion of there being a promised land… a land visible only from the pinnacle of a mountain. King – in his dream had been there, teetering on that precipice that gave clear view of the landscape below. It was there. He could see it –the Promised Land. He could visualize what it would be like…and how the dream would come real.

For those who were there, there was a stillness that was quite uncommon at Dr. King's speeches.

As the lines were delivered, there were several interruptions for applause. People shouted "Amen" in agreement with his comments and then came the most memorable moment of the speech. At the end, as his tempo and volume increased, he slowed his pace ever so slightly – yet he kept the rolling timbre of his voice and bellowed the final lines.

Dr. King began talking about the uncertain days ahead. He talked about the threats against his life – but lamented that it did not matter. He talked of not making it to that beautiful place he had seen in his dreams, resigned to the foretold ending.

"Mine eyes have seen the glory of the coming of the Lord"

The applause was deafening. The mood of this crowd had been elevated to heights unseen throughout the turmoil. These were ordinary people who were doing the extraordinary. They were people whose strength and courage and belief in Dr. King and his lieutenants would propel them to a greater role in American history. There was the continuing hope that things would change. The people were actually able to see it for themselves – that 'Promised Land' that King so eloquently described. They were now prepared, but not for what was about to happen less than 24 hours later. No one could have been prepared for that.

After the speech King held a series of meetings with the black leadership in Memphis. He even met with The Invaders, trying to persuade them all that the best possible way was the nonviolent way. The next morning at breakfast some of us were sitting around the table in the Peabody, and my friend asked me, "Ozell, didn't Martin seem very strange to you last night in his speech?"

I said, "No, you know Martin knows how to reach his audience."

But my friend said, "I know, but his whole language was different." I said, "Come to think about it, that's the first time I ever heard him chronicle this whole involvement in the civil rights movement," as if he wanted to make sure it was on record. He developed it all the way from Montgomery to the time he got stabbed in Chicago, you remember, and led all the way through Birmingham and up from Selma.

He chronicled all these things, but then he said, "but I'm not worried now." It was a resignation, it was that strange. We concluded after that King had a premonition of his death. Well, he just knew at some time or another he was going to be killed. They killed Ghandi. They killed Kennedy, and he had to know they were going to kill him. He knew it, yet he had no choice but to do what he was doing. King used to say the man who has not found something for which he's willing to die is yet to find something worth living for.

I harbored those thoughts as I continued to do my work in Memphis. I did not want Martin to die. His death would be a mighty blow to the movement. Yet still I knew there were others who could, if they would, step up and fill any void left by any member who was fallen. Again I raise this point. The movement was about so much more than Dr. King. There were thousands upon thousands of leaders large and small. Some held important positions; others were simply foot soldiers who would rise to the occasion whenever called upon. Each was important to this period of history. The records may never reflect all of the names and stories of the people who made a difference...but they knew it and they would have to tell their own story over the dinner table, or at a school or at a church service. I only wish there was a compendium of each and every story. I am sure it would fill volumes too numerous to print.

I especially wanted no harm to come to Martin under my watch. Not while I was there as a representative of the federal government. I also knew there was only so much that I could do to help protect this man and keep all of the participants safe. The evil in the world was simply too great. We were up against the enemies we knew and the enemies we could not see. Some of them were in uniform. Some of them held public office. Some of them even looked like me. On a crowded street filled with marchers or in a church service or in a small town or a metropolitan city, there was always danger and always a risk for harm.

When King first arrived in Memphis, he was staying at the Holiday Inn Riverfront. He moved to the Lorraine Hotel because of the complaints from The Invaders, who claimed King was staying in a so-called "white hotel." They said he didn't have any business staying there and needed to move across town to the Lorraine where black folk stayed. And he did.

Dr. King was registered in room 306 of the Lorraine.

When Martin moved to the Lorraine, we had to move too. I was staying in the Peabody. But we moved into room 308 of the Lorraine. I kept my room in the Peabody too, because that was the only way to get some rest. I knew I wouldn't get any rest at the Lorraine, although I would stay there until after the mass meeting. Afterwards, I would go back to the Peabody because we couldn't get telephone messages at the Lorraine. It might be the next day before I would get my messages. Somebody called yesterday, but there'd seemingly be nobody on the switchboard today. Since I was with the Department of Justice, I really did have to be reachable. I would always call the Peabody to see if I had messages. That's the way my staff in Washington kept up with me.

Dr. King really had a rigorous day, but he was getting ready to go to dinner with a local minister just a few minutes before 6 o'clock.

About that time, I went and got both newspapers – they had two papers in Memphis. I went into my room and turned on the TV. I kicked off my shoes and planned to get some rest between 6 p.m. and 7:30 p.m., the time the mass meeting was scheduled to start. It had been a most tiring day for me as well. As I pulled my shoes off and turned the TV on to get comfortable, I heard a shot ring out. I was not particularly upset by the shot because there was a lot of shooting and fighting between The Invaders and the police. It appeared to be nothing unusual. But then I heard people clamoring down in the courtyard. At that time the parking lot was gravel, not paved the way it is now. So this movement of people below caused such a noise. I could hear people running through the courtyard. I said, "Let me get up here and see what in the world is going on."

I got up and came out of my room onto the balcony. I thought what had occurred was down in the courtyard because that's where the people were running. But they were running to get up where I was. As I peeked over the rail, they started to come up by the rail, up the steps toward me. I then realized whatever had occurred had happened upstairs. As I looked around about 3 or 4 paces from me was King's body. He was slumped back against the wall. I froze momentarily – not wanting to believe what I had seen. This man of peace moments ago was so full of life, laughing and joking with his friends. He had delivered one of the best speeches of his life just hours earlier and now this. Blood-stained pavement and all the elements he had fought to prevent – violence and harm to people had now been leveled onto him.

One of the first people to get to him was my coworker Jim Laue. Jim ran to get a towel to try to stop his bleeding and by that time Jesse was there and a whole host of people. I didn't go over because there was no purpose. I could serve but to block off access for the ambulance. The ambulance came quickly and they picked him up and carried him to the hospital. I got in my car and went to the hospital, too. I went directly to the night administrator and told them who I was. I identified myself and showed my credentials and told him I needed to find out how Dr. King was because I had to report to my agency. I knew other people in the Justice Department, and especially those in community relations service were looking to hear from me. In short order, the administrator arrived. He walked swiftly and escorted me down to the emergency room. He didn't allow me to enter the E.R., but he took me to an outer room and asked a group of doctors if somebody would come out and brief me as to Dr. King's condition. One doctor came out, looked me straight in the eye and said, "He's dead, Mr. Sutton." At that moment it seemed as if time was standing still. It seemed for a while that I was moving in slow motion until I quickly realized that I was on the job. My soul was shaken, my worst fears were realized, but I had a job to do. I had to move into action. There would be time for grieving, crying and wondering what would come next. But right then, I had a responsibility to the government of the United States. Only a minute or so had passed – but my mind raced – though I was not moving.

That was an awful night. I ran and got on the phone quickly because I knew the lines were going to get tied up. But I was able to get through to Roger Wilkins, our director at that time. I got through to Roger, and Roger quickly got the Attorney General, who was Ramsey Clark at that time. Ramsey notified President Johnson at the White House and soon the federal government sprang into action. At a time when it seemed that things moved slowly in D.C., this was a time when all hands were called on deck because there was no question what would happen next. Clark was ordered by the president to board a plane and fly to Memphis to lead the investigation into finding Dr. King's killer. The president offered any and all assistance the government could muster, including the U.S. military, although everyone hoped it would never come to that.

The King entourage acted just like the disciples did when Christ went to the cross. Andy, Jesse, Jose and Ralph David Abernathy and I – the whole gang – walked around in a daze, not quite knowing what to do. My immediate concern was for the safety of the thousands of people who were King's followers. We went over to the Mason Temple hall, a big temple owned by the sanctified church that could seat about 15,000 people. I went over there, even though that was not my prerogative to do that. The hall was full. Everyone there knew King had been shot, and by now they just learned that he was dead. They were just sitting there. I could hear a pin fall even with all those people sitting there. Their faces spoke of their hurt, their loss. Their tears rolled down their cheeks and dripped onto their clothes. Those tear-filled eyes looked vacant – empty, full of worry, fear, hurt and anger. Their King was dead. Their hopes had been vested in the promises of his words; in the resonance of his voice; in the surety, the confidence he exuded. Change would come. But not today, though. This was a time to grieve for the precious life that disappeared in a fraction of a second.

I went to the microphone and announced that I knew they had been informed that Dr. King had been shot and is now dead, but I advised them to go straight home. "There's nothing you can do tonight, and I'm sure that your leadership will be getting together tomorrow to decide whatever is to be done. That will be announced, so I would suggest you go straight home." And they did. They got up and filed out just as quietly as they entered. That was an awful night.

My wife reached me by telephone about 2 a.m. Of course, she had been on pins and needles about my welfare, because she knew wherever the accident was, I was there. I had friends calling from all over the country that night trying to find me. A lady from a little town called Jonesboro, Arkansas who I'd known when I directed the Arkansas Council was among them. She was a member of my board, and she was frantically trying to find me. She finally found me later that night at about 4 o'clock in the morning in the Peabody Hotel, and she said "Ozell?"

I said, "yes."

"Are you alright?"

I said, "I am fine, thank you."

She said, "Well I've called every place I know in Memphis – I bet you I've made 20 calls to Memphis, trying to find you."

I said, "It sure is nice to have friends like you." And she said "Well, you know when it comes to you, I was concerned, and I just knew you were somewhere close, because that's just like you." And I said, "Yeah, I was too close." And I talked to my wife too. My wife would always accuse me of not telling her a lot of things when danger was involved. I just didn't want to tell her because I didn't want her to worry. I guess when you're away from a person; you worry more than the person who is perhaps facing danger because you don't know what's going. I didn't tell my wife and my children quite often what things were really like. It was only later when they found out what the circumstances were really like that night. They also learned of the stories of violence and near violence on other occasions during the Memphis crisis. I just didn't talk about it too much because I knew if every time I left home to go there, then I'd have to reveal information that could frighten them. I'd rather not do that. I was a different kind of person, even before I was with this agency. Even before I was dealing with civil rights issues, I never carried my children with me, unlike most people. It's hard for me to be nonviolent when you twist my child's arm, but you can twist mine.

Soon after King's death, word spread across the country. I could only imagine what people were thinking – how sad they must feel – how dashed their hopes were. Robert Kennedy was on the campaign trail and announced to supporters who had gathered at a rally to hear him speak – the news of King's assassination. Here is what he said to his supporters:

Indianapolis, Indiana
April 4, 1968

I have bad news for you, for all of our fellow citizens, and people who love peace all over the world, and that is that Martin Luther King was shot and killed tonight.

Martin Luther King dedicated his life to love and to justice for his fellow human beings, and he died because of that effort.

In this difficult day, in this difficult time for the United States, it is perhaps well to ask what kind of a nation we are and what direction we want to move in. For those of you who are black—considering the evidence there evidently is that there were white people who were responsible—you can be filled with bitterness, with hatred, and a desire for revenge. We can move in that direction as a country, in great polarization—black people amongst black, white people amongst white, filled with hatred toward one another.

Or we can make an effort, as Martin Luther King did, to understand and to comprehend, and to replace that violence, that stain of bloodshed that has spread across our land, with an effort to understand with compassion and love.

For those of you who are black and are tempted to be filled with hatred and distrust at the injustice of such an act, against all white people, I can only say that I feel in my own heart the same kind of feeling. I had a member of my family killed, but he was killed by a white man. But we have to make an effort in the United States; we have to make an effort to understand, to go beyond these rather difficult times.

My favorite poet was Aeschylus. He wrote: "In our sleep, pain which cannot forget falls drop by drop upon the heart until, in our own despair, against our will, comes wisdom through the awful grace of God."

What we need in the United States is not division; what we need in the United States is not hatred; what we need in the United States is not violence or lawlessness; but love and wisdom, and compassion toward one another, and a feeling of justice toward those who still suffer within our country, whether they be white or they be black.

So I shall ask you tonight to return home, to say a prayer for the family of Martin Luther King, that's true, but more importantly to say a prayer for our own country, which all of us love—a prayer for understanding and that compassion of which I spoke.

We can do well in this country. We will have difficult times; we've had difficult times in the past; we will have difficult times in the future. It is not the end of violence; it is not the end of lawlessness; it is not the end of disorder.

151

But the vast majority of white people and the vast majority of black people in this country want to live together, want to improve the quality of our life, and want justice for all human beings who abide in our land.

Let us dedicate ourselves to what the Greeks wrote so many years ago: to tame the savageness of man and make gentle the life of this world.

Let us dedicate ourselves to that, and say a prayer for our country and for our people.

For several weeks, I stayed in Memphis. There was much work to be done. We needed to ensure that the rights of citizens remained intact and that when and where we could, we could keep violence from erupting. All across the country there had been reports of violence. Some of the worst was in major cities like Chicago, Baltimore and Washington D.C. Federal troops were called upon to quell the violence and rioting. Leaders called for calm, but it fell on deaf ears. For weeks, there were rumblings large and small. They eventually died down, but there continued to be a seething underneath as King was buried and the investigation into his assassin, James Earl Ray, continued.

RETURN TO
LITTLE ROCK

It seems sometimes that everything happens at once. I was busy working with the assembled government agencies in Memphis. I, too, was continuing in my role as a liaison between the local government and black leaders. In the midst of all this, I received a phone call from a familiar voice, Winthrop Rockefeller. The death of Dr. King had the entire nation reeling and re-evaluating the condition of Blacks in the country. People raised questions about whether we had made progress and whether the movement was in vain. It was now time to see if whites were truly sympathetic and understanding of our plight. In Little Rock, residents raised questions about the lack of representation in the higher levels of state government. Leaders were taking Governor Win Rockefeller to task. After all, he had the power to make changes. It had been suggested to the governor to call Ozell Sutton and ask for his advice and input.

There had been a rally of sorts at the state capitol in Little Rock, presumably to commemorate Dr. King's passing. When it was over, Winthrop Rockefeller locked arms with the people assembled there and sang the song of freedom – "We Shall Overcome!" Local leaders asked the governor to appoint a black special assistant and advisor. This position would report directly to the governor and assist him in reaching those goals of more blacks in higher positions in state government.

I was delighted to hear from my old friend and former employer.

"Ozell, this is Winthrop Rockefeller!"

"What is the occasion of the great governor of Arkansas calling me?"

"Well, Ozell, don't be surprised. We always had a good relationship. Let me get right to the point. The Black leaders here have asked for this position of special assistant to the governor. I asked them who they wanted to take the position and they said you!"

I have to admit that I was taken by surprise at the call and the offer. I had been engrossed in the events of the day and surely didn't see this coming. I replied to the governor, "Well, I don't know Mr. Rockefeller. I am here in Memphis – it is important that I be here."

He asked, "When are you coming home?"

"I actually will be home to see my family this weekend."

"While you are here, come by the mansion and see me"

I hung up the phone and began to contemplate what I should do and how I would respond to the offer from a man who had not only been my employer, but my friend.

The weekend arrived and I was happy to be back home. My first agenda item was to hold and kiss my wife and three girls. I surely had missed them after being there in Memphis amid all the turmoil and the awfulness of the situation. Holding my children always gave me a fresh perspective on things. It helped to cleanse my mind and make me realize the importance of my work. I know they would be happy for me to take this job. It would mean I would be home more. I liked the idea, too. Also, I knew I had a responsibility and a gift that had to be shared not just in Little Rock, but wherever I was needed. There is a funny thing about realizing your calling. You never know where it will take you or when you will be needed. The best you can do is try to keep a level head, and not overanalyze your life, and allow our God above guide your steps. In short, sometimes you have to pray for answers and guidance. And that is just what I did.

I made the call to the governor that weekend and went as requested to his massive and well-appointed home. Four columns adorned the front of the mansion and stretch up to the federal style gable at the top. A sweeping vista inside led your eyes up a grand staircase that eventually wound to the second floor. A crystal chandelier anchored the space at the upper landing. In short order, the familiar face of the governor appeared, and he welcomed me to his home.

Winthrop once again gave me the background of his predicament, and thus the rationale for his telephone call to me in Memphis.

I told him I would join him and take the position, but only on leave from the Justice Department. I asked him to go to Washington to talk with U.S. Attorney General Ramsey Clark. I knew the governor and the attorney general could make this happen. I wanted Rockefeller to let Clark know how important it was for me to be in Little Rock. I knew we could make some great changes in the state. We were able to get as much done over a cup of coffee than over the table of a big meeting with lots of people. I had done it before and was prepared to use the same skills again. The governor knew this. I had a network. My work as a reporter with the Arkansas Democrat, voter registration all over the state and my NAACP work made me well suited for the position.

Mr. Winthrop made good on my request and promptly boarded his private plane and flew to Washington to meet with Attorney General Clark. I saw myself in a good position. The governor had come to me and offered me a job I had not applied. I viewed it as being in a posture of strength – not strength for myself, but for my people.

The meeting in Washington went well and I was hired. Of course, I had other demands of the governor before we sealed the deal. I insisted on being able to interact with the governor without having to go through anybody – not secretaries – not assistants. I wanted unfettered access. He agreed.

I also insisted it be well known I was in a high position. The governor had no problem with that and in fact gave me the third best office in the building.

I remember once a white employee at the capitol asked me, "How can you be that close to the governor and you did not come up through the ranks."

I could not contain my arrogance, "The difference is that you applied for a job. I did not. The governor came to me and that gave me a leg up on you!" She was not amused.

The governor made sure I was well-compensated and on par to his executive director's salary. There was no budget for my position since it was created by the governor. So, he and his brothers paid my salary and benefits because requests to the state legislature to fund my job failed.

I went to work immediately examining the positions in state government that were vacant or soon to be vacated. I also compiled a list of people who would be well-suited for those positions. I asked the governor to give me the next five appointments. I tried to fill a seat on the state school board. I sent three names to them. The first two were turned down by the senate, including a black man by the name of John Walker, a young lawyer and graduate from the law school at Yale University. Next, I tried William Henry Townsend, a local optometrist. He too was denied. I finally submitted the name of a young Episcopal priest by the name of Washington. He was lesser known and was approved with no problem.

Next, I wanted a black on the board of the state police, the state planning commission, the welfare board and the Office of Equal Opportunity. This would be no small undertaking. Even with the support and the governor, many of these positions had to be approved by the legislature. The governor's relationship with them already was a bit tenuous so it came as no surprise there were many who were in opposition to giving this kind of power to black people. In addition, Winthrop Rockefeller was still trying to rebuild the reputation of Little Rock as a place that was welcoming to all people. He had been left with an awful legacy carved by Orval Faubus who in his term in office had been vocal about his opposition to equal rights for Negro people. His snubbing of President Eisenhower during the integration of Central High School and his handling of the violence that occurred had caused businesses that otherwise would have come to Arkansas – to locate in other states. Win Rockefeller had the name recognition, the business savvy and a political acumen to make change occur. However, he had to erase the vestiges of the past and ensure the citizen and future business associates the state was in fact on the mend and improving.

I was particularly proud of one hire, Sonny Walker. Sonny was a self-proclaimed radical, but he knew how to get things done and he had a lot of experience in the area of human rights. He was a product of Little Rock schools and was raised with the thousands of other black children who endured the turbulent times of integration and racism. Like many people of his day, he had become hardened to the injustices that had made his life and the lives of others yearn for a chance to be involved and to make a difference. Sonny Walker had committed his life to the movement. At the time I called him, he was already working for a state agency as the directors for the local community action agency similar to the well-known Economic Opportunity Agency, EOA. Sonny and I had talked about his coming to work for the state and he expressed excitement at the prospect. We knew full well what was happening at the time. We were keenly aware that we were making history. We were breaking ground and shattering barriers that heretofore had been impossible to surpass. This was the beginning of a revolution of sorts; a realization for those who lived in this area that change was here. Change was here to stay.

After a number of discussions everything was set. We were prepared to make the call to Sonny Walker and ask him to become the first black man to sit on the governor's cabinet.

The call to Sonny was placed by Bob Faulkner who was the governor's chief of staff. He explained that Winthrop Rockefeller was interested in adding Sonny to his staff and would be honored if he would come in for an interview. This, of course, was a formality because the decision had already been made. Sonny had been prepped by me and told exactly what to expect. This was indeed one of my proudest moments. This was the kind of power that many people hear about – but never see. It is the kind of power that shapes administrations and builds politicians and puts a public face on the action that is so often bantered about a campaign folly or promises made before groups of people to quell their anger and give them a glimmer of hope that they too can influence change. This was for real. Sonny Walker was about to become the first black man appointed by a Southern governor to sit on the top tier of state authority and control people and dollars that had for years escaped our grasp.

Sonny was delighted to be a part of this history and the governor showed his desire to make this appointment happen no matter the cost. Sonny was already making a good salary at the time. The state had imposed a cap on salaries such that no state employee would make more than $15,000. This would have amounted to a pay cut. Sonny needed $2,500 more. The governor agreed and made arrangements through his personal foundation to make up the difference. Sonny received two checks, including one from the state and another from the Winthrop Rockefeller Foundation. Rockefeller used his personal money to make this significant change in Arkansas history. In so many ways, his actions demonstrated an uncompromising commitment to equality and fair treatment for people of color. It was hard finding those who were altruistic in their actions. Of course, Winthrop Rockefeller was a politician, but he was a different kind of politician. First and foremost, he did not need his job. He was wealthy nearly beyond measure. He had very little to personally gain, especially since his actions would subject him to ridicule from his white counterparts.

I could feel proud to realize what role I really played in the history of blacks in Arkansas. Sonny Walker has often spoken very kindly about me to others.

"There was hardly anything that dealt with relationships in the community that Ozell didn't have some role in. We have always been close personal friends. We also worked very hard to make ways for advancement of black people whenever and wherever we could. After I was well established with the Rockefeller administration, I was allowed to see even more areas where improvements could be made. In the years that would follow, Ozell and I co-chaired the initiative to integrate the staff at the television and radio station. We had no black reporters or anchors at any of the stations. Three T.V. stations and a host of radio stations and none employed blacks as on-air personalities. As a result of our efforts, all three stations hired blacks to be on air. The same held trued for radio stations like KOKY. We called the general managers of the stations or their owners and made appointments with them to discuss the hiring of African Americans. Channels 11, 4 and 7 - we took our demands to them and we even discussed the possibility of one other station setting up a curriculum at Philander Smith to train students. The first guy they hired was from Arkansas State University. He was a young man named Rob Wiley and he worked for Channel 4. There were hesitations but they knew if they refused, we were ready to launch selective buying campaigns aimed at the station's advertisers. We reminded them that we had done the same thing with the local banks. I remember one

general manager telling us, 'I don't mind hiring a negra – but you gotta find me someone qualified. I am not hiring someone just because they are a negra.' So we found Linda Torrence and she was hired for the position of public affairs at Channel 5.

We checked in on the first woman hired as a bank teller. We had met with the president of the First National Bank, B. Finley Vinson. We were concerned because the only black teller told us that she was being harassed. When she would go to the break room to have her lunch, she would discover that someone had put garbage in her food. Some of the white males in the bank felt as if they could take certain liberties with her. We were able to get that harassment stopped.

Ozell and I met with the Chamber of Commerce and their group '50 for the Future'. These were prominent business leaders who thought they spoke for the community. We told them their member businesses had to do better. There were no blacks selling cars or working in the grocery stores. We told them they had to hire more black people. We were not well received. So we organized young people to come to the stores and demonstrate. We told blacks that we do not recommend buying in stores where they did not hire blacks. Everything had to be targeted. Just because you made progress in one area – didn't mean that you were successful in others. We rallied black and white professionals in all areas to help in civil disobedience. We rallied for better teacher pay and the hiring of black police officers. Support for our efforts was not limited to Arkansas. All across the south people heard of and knew the name Ozell Sutton. This man, my friend, my confidante was fearless when it came to his engagement in matters to eradicate racial barriers.

– William "Sonny" Walker

My Past Comes Back to Visit Me

There were many occasions when I would sit in my office just a few steps from the most powerful office in all of Arkansas. I was always within an earshot of the governor and thanks to him I had unencumbered access to him at all times. This occurred for a number of reasons not the least of which was because we had a strong personal friendship and an abiding respect for each other on the job. I never abused my access and always held Win Rockefeller in the highest professional regard. He had done for blacks what no other politician had done. He had opened the door and allowed historic changes to happen and he valued the advice of those who were closest to him. Win Rockefeller liked people who were self-starters. He liked the people he empowered to handle problems or issues without the burden of his advice.

One day I was walking through the reception area and heard the receptionist say, "I'm sorry Mr. Holthoff, but Mr. Rockefeller is not in the office today. I stopped in my tracks. I could not believe my ears and was even more startled when my eyes fell upon the person she was addressing. There he was – right there in the governor's office. It was old man Holthoff, Claude Holthoff. He was the owner of the Holthoff Plantation where I was born and where my mama had toiled and labored. That Holthoff. He was standing there, but now he needed a cane to hold him upright. Time had weathered his body and no doubt arthritis had him in its painful grip. The same man Lula Belle had yelled at in the store some thirty years ago when she tried to sell her last bale of cotton. This was the man who had accused my mother of owing him money and thus was prepared to deny her the ability to sell what was rightfully hers. He was standing right there.

The receptionist asked him if he would like to meet with one of the governor's assistants. He replied, "Yes, I would." This was my cue. The receptionist turned and saw me standing there and said, "Mr. Sutton, can you see Mr. Holthoff?"

"Of course, I can, right this way sir." As I walked him toward the office area, memories of what transpired years ago came rushing to the forefront of my mind. The images were as clear as if they had happened moments ago, and the sound of his voice resonated as if he was speaking right now. Mr. Holthoff had thrown us off of his land after the dispute with my mama and we were left with no place to go – no place to call home. This was my chance to be in charge of his wishes and welfare like he had once been in charge of mine.

Rather than take Mr. Holthoff to my small office, I instead took him right into the governor's grand space. I took the liberty to positioning myself behind the governor's desk. It was a massive and magnificent hand carved piece of furniture given to the governor by one of his brothers when he took office. I sat there as if it were my own. I topped it off by plopping down into the impressive leather chair.

With an air of authority befitting someone sitting behind such a grand desk, I inquired, "What may I help you with sir?"

When he began to speak it was clear to me that he had no idea who I was. He started by introducing himself – telling me his name and he was just about to tell me where he was from when I interrupted, "You are from Gould!"

He was clearly caught off guard and stammered – "You know me?"

"Yes sir, I do," I replied.

"How do you know me?"

"Well sir, I was born in Gould on your place. Think back many years ago...a black widowed woman with a house full of children was a sharecropper on the Holthoff Plantation. Her name was Lula Belle. I am Lula Belle's youngest boy!"

For me the moment of silence between our voices was like an eternity. It was an uncomfortable silence during which memories of the past came rushing back to him. You could see it on his face. The silence was broken when he said, "I'll be damned!" As the words were rolling off his tongue, he simultaneously rose from his uncomfortable perch and turned to leave without even telling me the nature of his visit to the governor's office.

I actually knew why he was there. I asked him to please stay and allow me to hear his request. Uncomfortable as it was for him, I rather enjoyed this moment. He proceeded to tell me about the flooding and tornado damage done to his farm and other properties in rural Gould and throughout Lincoln County. Crops had been destroyed and there was significant property damage. The farmers in the area were in need of a decree from the governor's office declaring the area a disaster area. This appeal would be taken to the White House where the President could offer federal assistance. I informed Mr. Holthoff that I would return to the Gould area the next day, survey the damage and report back to the governor. The next day I took the governor's personal plane and flew into Pine Bluff. When I touched down Mr. Holthoff met me there. He boarded the plane and I ordered the pilot to give us the tour of the area as Holthoff directed us. Of course, we flew over his plantation. It looked different from up here – yet still hauntingly familiar. During the fly over, I remember my family working from sunup to sundown and receiving very little pay in return. I remember the trees and houses and the little landmarks that seemed insignificant to me then. As I looked, even the old stumps bring back memories. I remember this man sitting next to me arguing with my mother and the pain it brought to her. I had never seen my mother so mad at anyone as she had been at Mr. Holthoff. But the times had changed. My family had been in debt to the Holthoff Plantation and now it has come full circle. This time it was he and his property that was now in need – and soon to be indebted to me. To drive one more stake into this man's heart, I casually pointed out the ramshackle house where my family once lived.

I returned to Little Rock and talked with the governor about the devastation I saw and without hesitation he declared the area a disaster. Federal funds were on their way. I wondered how Lula Belle would respond if she could have been in her baby boy's shoes. For some reason, I doubt she would have been as diplomatic.

Perhaps old man Holthoff would still be sitting in the outer lobby – or perhaps she would have cursed him out again right there in the governor's office. I learned through that experience that it makes no sense to fight with your past. The punches have nowhere to land. You will get exhausted from the effort and frustrated; the ending is always the same. Sometimes it is better to let it be. Don't forget it, but just let it be and move on because your today will soon be your past.

THE JOB:
HELPING TO DEFINE C.R.S.

I encountered many other incidents of my involvement in the movement. I found it possible to make significant changes and avert tragedies through the power of my official position with the Justice Department. My work remained behind the scenes and out of the sight of a camera's lens. No one had television cameras on the street corners, in the dark alleys and churches, and open fields where I negotiated a fragile peace during the most turbulent of times, and in some of the most obscure of places. It has been decades since some of the following incidents took place, but they are strung together with familiar faces that always appeared where they were needed. The common thread has always been that wherever we were, people were oppressed. We were always in a place that was like a tinderbox that required only a small spark of controversy to set it ablaze. Staffers of the Office of Community Relations were always aware that their presence did not guarantee peace. Instead, we were the eyes and ears of the federal government. We were the pipeline to and from Washington where elected officials were always concerned that something bad could happen under their watch. It was in their best interest that no harm came to citizens no matter the color of their skin. As altruistic as their actions might have appeared, political capital was always at stake. When we needed action quickly, we used those stakes as a valuable bargaining chip. Local politicians too, practiced calculating the risk of violence under their watch. They were always concerned about how they would be perceived in the court of public opinion. They knew history would judge them for the decisions they made under pressure and the end results of their actions. There always was a price to be paid when people were oppressed and fought to change the course of their lives. It may be violence, which could lead to bad publicity and scrutiny from outsiders. There was the financial consideration too. They had to decide whether to spend the money to protect demonstrators and those who held counter demonstrations. They weighed the potential economic loss if businesses were harmed and consumers ceased shopping. They stayed away from the areas of confrontation and many times they stayed at home when a highly publicized event would take place. Local, state, federal officials faced these potential liabilities. For me and my people, it was a powerful asset. It was the one thing that everyone understood: money. In the final analysis, money and political capital came down to the same thing. The following chapters give you a sense of what we were able to do in the business of protecting people's rights. My credentials with the Department of Justice were no guarantee of my personal safety. My brushes with death did not stop when I returned. But it was all worth it. It was my job. It was my passion. It was the continuation of my calling and my contribution to the history of the United States of America.

I guess the best way to describe what we did in CRS is to understand that we had no written rule book. We had no game plan except that we wanted to keep the peace wherever and whenever we could. Following the assassination of King, CRS broadened its efforts to focus on simply responding to crisis and trying to address the causes of racial conflict. The mission was now one of being proactive – trying to get ahead of the problems – before they manifested into violence. It would require willing minds, hearts and listening ears.

Former director of CRS, Roger Wilkins led the agency from 1966 to 1969. His uncle was Roy Wilkins, who was a longtime president of the NAACP. Roy Wilkins followed W.E.B. Dubois as editor of The Crisis, which is the official magazine of the NAACP. Roy would later serve as the executive secretary of the NAACP; and in 1964, he became the organization's first executive director.

Roger followed in his family's tradition and offered himself to serve others. He was appointed to the U.S. Attorney General's Office and is a professor at George Mason University in Fairfax, Va. Wilkins describes the CRS like this:

> *"My theory was that our job was not to be the fireman and run into a place, water people down, and send them home. That didn't make anything better- you just handled a little flare up.*
>
> *The underlying problem in our view, was the unfairness of American society and that in order to do anything meaningful about cities – you had to try to get the cities to engage the program of leveling the playing field and that is what we tried to do. So in a lot of places it worked.*
>
> *There is a difference between Corporate America then and now. Back in the 60's – major corporations like U.S. Steel and Ford had roots in major cities. The heads of those corporations had a stake in the city themselves. They may have grown up there and even before the riots these companies turned their attention from building a museum to closing the gap between blacks and whites. They tried to establish a local mechanism that focused on jobs, housing, educa-tion, and also the police. These are areas where the disparities caused*

the sparks that blew up into the full blown riots. I think most of America looked at the riots as the problems themselves and we looked at the underlying problems.

The underlying problems; the lives of our people have for centuries been hampered by the underlying problems. Unseen, these were issues that people in power chose never to acknowledge or to understand. Throughout the movement all that was ever asked was a fair consideration of our conditions, consider our circumstance and make amends to level the playing field. At every turn we sought to achieve racial balance and harmony through an understanding of these issues and to encourage those in leadership to address them as a way of preventing violence. Sometimes it is difficult to get people to buy into theories without any documented proof or a willingness to see an ideal as plausible and possible. I lived through some of the same conditions that caused people to riot. I have been the victim of racism and I have spent a life in the minority. I also know what it means to look at a situation with objective eyes and to develop solutions for the common good. Protecting life and liberty and property is only a temporary fix, a band-aid. We want to address that which lies beneath much like the root of a plant with it tentacles stretching in several directions in search of sustenance and nutrients and water and all those elements that are essential to life. I view that as a vital role of CRS.

It has often been my belief that there has to be a better way. It seems that the Community Relations Service is called into conflicts when conditions are just that – conflicts teetering on the edge of violence. It would be great if we were not needed – that the conditions for people around the country did not have to escalate to a point where there is potential violence. But we do not live in a perfect world. We exist here as people of diverse backgrounds and beliefs and often those beliefs place one group in superiority to another – or at least – that is their belief. Human rights are often the last thing considered. Individual rights are often the first.

Regardless of how it starts, the CRS is there when called to ensure that things end peacefully. I had served as the Southern regional director of CRS since 1965 and had been involved in hundreds of cases either in the field or dispatching staff to hotspots. We covered a wide territory including the states of Alabama, Georgia, Kentucky, Mississippi, North Carolina, South Carolina and Tennessee. Every case we were involved in was different, but each had similar patterns – similar themes. There were always several components with which to deal. They included the two parties in disagreement- more often than not it was black against white. There was law enforcement, religious groups, elected officials and then there were those who were not involved but could have been impacted by the activities of the parties involved. So many times there were the townspeople, who did not take sides, but the controversy was right there in their neighborhoods or involved the people next door and that put them at risk. We had to protect everyone – no matter what side they were on.

INTERLUDE

I have tried to maintain some sense of time and chronology throughout this passage, and I will continue to do so. I dealt with so many cases in my professional career and incidents in my private life that it is somewhat difficult to place each one in its proper time continuum. Another issue was that there were few records kept of where we were and what we were doing in any particular case. The CRS was still in its infancy and we were basically writing the operating manual in real time. We had to improvise and be willing to think fast on our feet. Lives were at stake and in the heat of the moment; no manual would give you the perfect solution to some of the problems we faced. I will share significant information that will not follow a particular timeline. In my earlier chapters, I created vignettes of my life. That practice will continue with the telling of the stories that shall follow.

It is important to note that there were a number of people in the CRS who were vital to our relative success. Like me, many of them were not new to the role of being a conciliator; however we forged new territory in the early days of this agency. There is an old adage that when you start naming people, you will likely leave someone out. In advance let me say if I have omitted anyone, please chalk it up to my head and not to my heart.

These are the people who worked closest with me and I thank them for their dedication to our mission and their genuine concern for people. I thank them for their friendship and their loyalty to the agency and to me. They worked many long hard hours for average pay, but their reward is truly knowing that their actions saved lives and also changed the course of history. I salute you my good friends and thank you for being there for me, for the agency and for the people of America. A few of them are:

FRED CRAWFORD	LEON BURRUSSS
ERNEST JONES	ROBERT SHRAEDER
ERNEST STALLWORTH	THOMAS BATTLES
MARGARET CURET	ROBERT ENSLEY
DORIS PETTY	WARNER HUDSON
SUE BROWN	

CLARKSDALE, MISSISSIPPI

There were many nights when I would be alone on the road. The Office of Community Relations would occasionally send teams of facilitators into the field. I recall one circumstance in particular where I was in the company of two other people who were employed by the agency. It was 1964. There was a crisis in Clarksdale, Mississippi. My team went there to represent a federal presence and to conciliate racial differences.

Clarksdale is 105 miles southeast of Little Rock. It is tucked right there on the westernmost line of Mississippi in the northern portion of the state. If the name of this little hamlet seems familiar, then perhaps you know of it because of its rich history of the blues. This town was known for its incredible music. Some great performers were born here, including Sam Cooke, Ike Turner, John Lee Hooker. Today there are markers here commemorating this city's contribution to the blues. It also had a reputation for racial unrest and tension.

The great Thurgood Marshall had to take on one of this town's wealthiest attorneys who had argued for segregation in public schools. The case – Brown vs. Board of Education. Marshall argued before the United States Supreme Court and won – bringing an end to "separate but equal" accommodations in the U.S.

The city was not very far at all – but it was light years away from the kind of civility that existed between the races in Little Rock. There had been talk of some potential violence here as a result of disputes between blacks and whites.

When my team arrived we found that the Holiday Inn was the only hotel we knew of that was accepting black patrons and providing sleeping accommodations. Now even though the hotel accepted blacks, to my knowledge, they had not done so when we arrived. Perhaps they told us that because we were representing the Department of Justice. I took no comfort in knowing I would be the first black man to stay in this establishment.

We had done all we could that day including meeting with the local police, the government leaders, and the organizations who were in protest of their treatment. I was uneasy and I was tired. A good rest was earned but not to be realized on this night.

The word spread quickly around this small town that we were in the city. Three black men from out of town were there and some people didn't know why. All they knew was they were planning to sleep at the Holiday Inn. Tensions in town were high and the mob mentality was present. We checked into the hotel but soon thereafter trouble started. At first I was encouraged because there were a few black maids and maintenance people on the grounds. I became weary though by the look in their eyes. They were surprised to see black folk checking in. Their look was more one of worry. They knew something we didn't know and we hadn't the time to talk. As soon as we reached our rooms on the second floor, we heard a commotion outside. We peered out of the curtain to see members of the Ku Klux Klan in the parking lot. They were gathering quickly. Some of them were armed. Others had guns visible in their pickup trucks. We knew we were in danger.

One of the men in our group was from Michigan. He had never seen anything like this. I, on the other hand, had lived through similar experiences and had seen the terrible things that could happen to people who happen to be in the wrong place at the wrong time.

My coworker said to me, "What should we do? They have the hotel surrounded.

The other gentleman said, "Let's call the police!"

I responded, "Can't call the police! The police are Klan! If we call the police we are inviting the Klan into our room!"

We looked at each other with great concern.

The first friend said, "Well let's call the FBI!"

To which I responded, "Can't call the FBI. The FBI are Klan sympathizers!"

After a few moments, I said hand me the phone. I called down to the switchboard and gave the operator the phone number to the Department of Justice in Washington. Now even at that time, knowing I was a black man calling the DOJ – there was no guarantee that the people on the other end would move very quickly. If you thought Washington moved slow – it moved even slower for Black people.

After a few minutes, the call was made and was put through to our room. Now I had sense enough to know that whatever I said on that line was probably being monitored by the switchboard operator who may have a husband or relative in that mob just outside my window. Who knows, she may have allowed one of them to listen in.

I got the secretary on the line in Washington at my headquarters. I told that operator to find me a middle aged black man. It could be a janitor or anything, just any middle aged black man would do.

In short order, I heard a voice on the other end. It was in fact a man who happened to be sweeping the hallway just outside the office. When I was confident of whom I was speaking to, I said this, "OOH-DAY – OOH YAH – IX – SPAY PATEN-LAY...."

The man in turn answered me in Pig Latin. I knew we were in business. You see in those days we had a number of ways of talking to each other so that others around us couldn't understand. We had to do that. Code words, actions and symbols have been a part of our culture since well before the Underground Railroad, when symbols were used to announce to slaves the right time to run away and the direction in which they should go. These symbols were sewn onto quilts and were hung on the lines as if to dry. They were instead billboards announcing the time and place to run.

The man on the other end of the phone listened intently. I explained to him in as much detail as I could muster our situation. I told him we were in the Holiday Inn in Clarksdale, Mississippi. That we were surrounded by the Klan and Klan sympathizers and that we were surely in trouble.

This man was able to get the word to the Attorney General. At that time the A.G. was Ramsey Clark. Clark summoned U.S. Marshals into his office and sent word for them to contact the local field office and escort my coworkers and me to safety. In a manner of minutes 12 marshals arrived and knocked on our door. They called our names and we moved quickly to leave that hotel – never to stay there again.

DECATUR, ALABAMA

In 1978, Decatur, Alabama was town that was tediously growing more comfortable with the memories of its racially-charged past. The tensions here lived just below the apparent gentile charm exuded by most Southern cities. The civil rights movement was ten years in its past, the schools had integrated with no problem, but there never was a comfortable feeling between the races. It was in a sense – just a polite toleration of the differences in race. Blacks lived, attended church and socialized primarily with other blacks, the whites did the same. After all, this was a town thrust into the public eye in the 1930's when eight black youth were sentenced to death on a charge of raping two white women. They became known as "The Scottsboro Boys". They had been held in a jail in Scottsboro, Alabama after being accused of the most heinous of crimes of that time – the disturbance of the sanctity of the white South's most cherished and revered asset – white women.

The charges were trumped up when two women claimed they were raped by a gang of ten to twelve black boys – all in their teens. The young men who were arrested had been pulled off a freight train. They had been riding through the South looking for work at lumber mills and factories. None had been anywhere near the location of the alleged rapes. The trial and retrials and motions and hearings went on for decades. The Scottsboro Boys case was eventually labeled "The greatest miscarriage of justice in American History".

What happened on February 16, 1978 would conjure up memories of those horrible days as again – a black man was accused of raping a white woman. It was a case that escalated to three different charges of rape against the same man. All of the alleged victims were white. While this case would be different, its outcome was all too familiar, and the tension surrounding it was felt by anyone who lived through those terrible days.

It all started when twenty-five year-old Tommy Lee Hines was arrested in downtown Decatur. A woman claimed he was peeping into her office window and she called the police. In reality Tommy Lee had been looking for work. He had applied in the very office of the woman who had accused him of "peeping at her". He was merely standing on the street looking back at the building on the day after he had   been denied employment by this woman. Patrol cars were not far away and searched the street for a man fitting his description. Tommy Lee was found not far away filling out a job application at another place of business. Officers arrested him and placed him in a patrol car. One of the officers remarked that he fit the description of another suspect who was believed to have committed several rapes in the area. According to articles and testimony at the trial, Hines was read his rights and an officer asked him right there in the patrol car had he committed two or three rapes. Hines answered, "Three." The only problem is that Hines was illiterate, retarded and had an I.Q. of 39. He later would cryptically sign confessions to the crimes. They were confessions he could neither write nor read. His parents were not allowed to see him during questioning and officers ignored the claims by relatives that Tommy was impaired.

Word spread quickly and over time, while Tommy sat in a jail cell, other forces were at work to gain his freedom. There was so much attention given this case that it was moved from Decatur to a small town some 30 miles to the south, called Cullman in Cullman County. The Journal of the Southern Regional Council called *Southern Changes*, described Cullman County as a church going county where not a drop of legal liquor was sold for 50 miles. Less than one percent of the population was black and most of them lived in an area outside of town called "The Colony".

"We have our coloreds in the Colony down there" said one resident. "They're treated as good as any Whites. They just stick to their business and we stick to ours. Their kids go to school with our."

"I've sold cars to the niggers around here for years, said another man. "They pay on time just like the White folks." (*Tommy Lee Hines and the Cullman Saga* by Bob Dart – Southern Changes the Journal of the Southern Regional Council Vol. 1, No. 3, 1978, pp.12-15)

People in Decatur monitored every move in the case and organized protests both for and against this boy who barely understood what was happening and who had no sense that he was the center of a grave injustice. The NAACP was calling for the charges to be dropped, that there was no way this man could have confessed to crimes he could barely comprehend. The KKK called for quick justice and the execution of Tommy Lee Hines.

From our offices in Atlanta, we monitored the activities in Decatur. We knew that tensions were high and that we would eventually be called upon to assist in keeping the peace between two groups of people who for decades had clashed over the treatment of people and the protection of civil rights.

The call came from the Alabama State Patrol. Their intelligence revealed that there were expectations of unruly demonstrations and possible face to face confrontations between the NAACP and the KKK. I dispatched Ernie Jones and Robert Enseley to investigate. The first thing they discovered and reported to me was that the tiny town of Cullman was ill equipped to handle a large demonstration of any type, much less one that could lead to bloodshed. The city and the county had no parade ordinance. We knew it would take very little persuading of the local government to approve a plan that would lessen the possibility of dangerous confrontation.

My conciliators met with the city and county attorneys and drew up an ordinance which over time was adopted by other municipalities. It included items like requirements for parade permits, the control of parade routes by local government, and the conditions under which permits could be revoked and events cancelled in the interest of protecting people and property.

A week before the trial began there was a test of the wills of local and state law enforcement. Members of the KKK met in the town of Cullman. It was an unexpected gathering and there were only six to eight state troopers in the area. The hooded Klansmen confronted police, knowing they had them outnumbered. They refused to disperse but instead grew more agitated at police and eventually ran the troopers off with threats of violence and a visible display of weapons and manpower.

One week later the Klan planned another demonstration in hopes of ramping up residents just a day or two before the trial was to begin in earnest. This time the Alabama State Patrol was ready. At our urging their numbers had been increased and they were glad they did. This time the Klan tucked tail and left, except for a few die hard members. They were confronted by officers and when they refused to obey orders – they were beaten and arrested. This would be a precursor of the type of problems we would experience over the next week or so, both in Cullman and Decatur and points in between.

Once the trial started there were a few minor problems in Cullman. This mostly involved members of the KKK protesting outside the courthouse. They had billed their presence as that of concerned citizens trying to keep a vigil at a trial in which they had a vested interest. In fact most of them weren't from the area and some had been recently recruited into the Klan.

The bigger issues and protests took place in the town where the original "crime" had occurred, Decatur. Large protests were held there and there was representation by both the Klan and large civil rights groups including the NAACP, and the Southern Christian Leadership Conference, the SCLC. Local ministers had organized the protests and rallied people of color to send a message to the district attorney that they were displeased with this trial and this rush to judgment for a man who could not comprehend what was happening to him much less commit the crimes of which he was accused.

The mission of CRS was to approach this powder keg on several fronts. Marge Corrett was dispatched to Cullman. She was to monitor the trial and the atmosphere around it. She was to gather intelligence on the judge in the case. Jack Riley presided over the trial, and while he was friendly to our staff he was not overly helpful in providing information. Marge even had lunch with him on occasion and stayed in the same hotel as the judge and the jury. They had been sequestered throughout the trial to protect them from outside influences. The jury, by the way, was all white, nine men and three women.

Bob Ensley also was between Cullman and Decatur. Bob also would gather information from the local police as well as the black leaders who descended on these two small towns in an effort to organize and lead protests in both Cullman and Decatur.

We also set up a system for "rumor control". This was very important because often rumors did more harm than the truth. As soon as a rumor would start about possible violence or the names of people who might be coming to the area, we would quickly check the information out and tell everyone involved what we knew in an effort to keep emotions and actions in check. The CRS Staff also met with local law enforcement and city leaders. We assessed their ability to control crowds and their access to more help if needed.

The trial lasted for a week. There were several small skirmishes but there was always the potential for something much greater. Each group had their protests either in Decatur or in Cullman. The tensions really began to mount once the trial ended and the jury deliberations began. We did not have to wait long. After three hours of deliberations, the jury came back with a verdict; guilty on all counts. Tommy Lee Hines sat there with the same confused look he had displayed throughout the trial. He had listened to police officers, forensic specialists, psychiatrists, even relatives testify in his case – each offering their opinion or interpretation of fact to explain what happened and what could not have happened.

Those watching the case from Decatur to Cullman set things into motion for a large march the following Saturday. The SCLC announced immediately that it would be bringing thousands of people to Decatur. The Klan fired right back announcing it would disrupt any attempt to march.

The staff of the Southeast Region of the Community Relations Service moved its conflict resolution into full speed. The SCLC was firm in its conviction to march. The Klan planned to occupy the same streets at the same time. This was a recipe for disaster, neither especially since no one could predict the number of people who would be coming there nor would they know the motives for each.

There also was the issue of the Klan who had announced that it would be armed for its own protection. Upon hearing this some of the participants from the SCLC, who had vowed to cleave to its pledge of nonviolence began to murmur that they would be using any means necessary to protect themselves.

It was the opinion of the CRS staff that we could not depend on the Decatur Police department to protect the marchers and prevent violence. That was when I knew I needed to take the safety and security of everyone involved out of the hands of local authorities and put the issue within the purview of the State of Alabama. I asked for and received a meeting with then Governor George Wallace. I briefed the governor on the level of conflict we were expecting and shared with him our intelligence about the people involved and their intent. The governor agreed that the level of force needed to prevent the violence would have to be massive.

I told the governor we needed 300 troopers and four companies of the Alabama National Guard to augment the Decatur police and the county sheriff's deputies. He ordered the deployment of soldiers and troopers without hesitation. At the same time, we assisted the city council with the drafting of the ordinance requiring a permit to march. This would give the city and our people more control over the marchers. The ordinance also made it illegal to have firearms within 300 yards of a demonstration or march. This gave the city the authority to arrest anyone with a weapon near the march site and anywhere along the route.

The City of Decatur received the two requests for permits. The Klan would hold its march and rally beginning at 10 o'clock in the morning. The SCLC event would begin at 2 o'clock in the afternoon. This would allow the Klan to have its demonstration and clear the area long before the SCLC rally and march would begin. Governor Wallace had vowed to keep the peace. Somehow though, I was still uneasy about this whole thing. I kept hearing in my mind the threat by the Klan to come to the rally armed. We also knew that there would be observers from the opposing group. The only way for this to happen peacefully would be if both sides promised to appear unarmed, exercise their rights and leave peacefully. There needed to be a meeting with each group.

The day before the marches I was climbing the stairs at city hall. There I saw the Imperial Wizard of the KKK, Bill Wilkinson. I strode right up to Mr. Wilkinson and asked him if I could meet with him about this march and rally. Surprisingly, he agreed but had one condition. I had to meet with him alone – no staff – no police and the meeting had to take place in the headquarters of the local Klan chapter. I then surprised him by agreeing to go there.

I reported back to my staff and alerted them that the meeting was to take place that evening. Several of them tried to talk me out of going out there alone. You know they say that God protects babies and fools. Which do you think I was?

Now, I have to be totally honest with you. I would be lying if I said that I was not afraid. I certainly had a number of images running through my mind. You have seen the photographs of what the Klan can do to people. They had perfected domestic terrorism long before we knew what that meant. These were the people who rode through black neighborhoods in their white robes and tortured and murdered innocent black people. This was the organization that burned crosses in front yards and held hate-filled rallied in open fields on Saturday nights. This was the beast that led individuals to kill and maim and here I was about to walk right into their headquarters without an ounce of protection.

I drove myself to the outskirts of town to the location of their headquarters. A beer bellied armed man was standing there and chuckled as I closed the car door and walked up the stairs. Despite my fear, I was determined to be the professional I was and to perform my task without flinching.

I entered the tattered house and was met with the Southern Stars and Bars emblazoned on a wall. It was displayed there like an honorable tapestry from an ancient castle...only this was held up by thumbtacks on a paint peeled wall. I was searched for weapons and led down a hallway to a back room. There seated behind a desk was Bill Wilkinson. He did not rise to meet me but instead sat there and chuckled, "I'll be damned, you came!"

I returned with a slight chuckle myself, "I told you I would!"

"I didn't think you were fool enough to come out here all alone!" He sat there with a slight look of bewilderment.

"Now look Mr. Wilkinson, I came here to tell you that as a representative of the Department of Justice, I must enforce the law. You and your people are free to assemble, but you will not be allowed to bring anything at all that can be identified as a weapon. We have ordered federal troops, additional state troopers and other members of the Department of Justice will be there watching your every move. If we see a weapon or believe there are weapons on your person, you will be searched and you will be arrested! We will have enough law enforcement there to protect you and the other protestors. This will be a peaceful rally."

Wilkinson sat there and didn't respond at first. I guess he was thinking that if this fool is crazy enough to come out here all alone and unarmed then he will surely make good on his word to arrest me and anyone else who breaks the law. After a few moments he said you will not have any trouble out of my people. Half-heartedly believing him I said, "That would do well, Mr. Wilkinson, but I must emphasize that while I believe you are a man of your word, I know that I am. Leave any weapons you have here or you will be locked up! Good night sir!"

I rose on imitation steady legs and walked out the same way I came in. As I descended the stairs, I dare not look back, a sure sign that I was concerned. Instead I walked slowly, but with determination to the car, keys in hand. For half a second I wondered if someone had tampered with the car while I was inside. Click! The engine roared to life and I lowered the rental into gear, eased down on the accelerator and headed into town. My work was not finished this evening. I still had to meet with the other side of this rally; the hundreds of black protestors who themselves were readying for a confrontation.

Across town the Reverend Joseph Lowery was in the pulpit of a local church. Every pew was full and emotions were high. This was a typical pre-protest rally. The people here came to hear the facts as they knew them and to remind each other why they were there. This was all about one man who had been wrongly accused, tried, and convicted. This was for him and for others like him who had been the victim of a judicial system that was flawed in the eyes of black defendants. Reverend Lowery was eloquent in his delivery and drew shouts of "Amen!" and "That's right!" in agreement with his message. As the rally was slowing down, I asked Rev. Lowery to keep everyone in place and allow me to have a word with him and the other ministers in a back room.

As the congregation talked among themselves, I briefed the ministers on the plan for the following day. I impressed upon them as well to make sure that there were no weapons along the rally route. You have heard of 'gun-totin' preachers? Well these were some 'gun-totin' preachers, deacons, choir members – you name it. Now not everyone – but it was no secret that some of the marchers were on occasion armed – although nonviolence was emphasized at each of these similar gatherings. I instructed one of the local ministers to go out there and to be sure that when everyone came to the church the next day prior to the march – that they were to confiscate any weapons. We would have someone there to assist with this – with no questions asked. Otherwise we would have to arrest them as well. The ministers were all in agreement that this was the best course of action for the safety of everyone involved.

The next day hundreds of people showed up to participate in the march on behalf of Tommy Lee Hines. It is sad that his mental capacity could not allow him to comprehend the impact his case has had on people here and throughout the South. At the church quite a collection of weapons was confiscated, tagged and locked up while the rally progressed.

The National Guard was there. Local senators sent representatives; a large contingent of black state troopers was called into action. At that time the state was under a federal mandate that for every white trooper hired, two blacks had to be hired to raise the compliment of black state troopers.

This was no ill-advised event. We had an incredible contingency plan in place including the crucial element of rumor control. So often in situations like this the rumor mill would be in high gear. We would intercept as many of those rumors as possible and replace them with the truth. In fact we encouraged local people to call us with their concerns and we could put everything in its proper perspective. The rumors could be more dangerous than the truth and undermine the safety of people who are in attendance. We also had numerous city hall briefings and shared information among agencies. On this day we had a tense control on things.

The KKK came in large numbers as well. Our plan called for the protesters event to take place early in the day with the Klan and other demonstrators to take to the streets later and on a slightly different route. It worked. With the exception of a few rowdy people, things went as planned. A couple of shots had been fired – but at a distance from the protest and the shooter was promptly arrested. No one was hurt.

The next day the principal players in the rally were prepared to leave this small town. I would be flying into Huntsville, Alabama and Rev. Lowery and his party was flying back to Atlanta. I received word through our little intelligence network that members of the Klan were heading to the airport at the same time. We were told they took particular interest in the flight for Dr. Lowery. Our immediate concern was that there could be some type of explosive device on the plane. As a result we had the plane inspected closely. I also learned that at least two of the Klan members were booked on the same flight. I made a call to the chief of police, Lee P. Brown. Brown acknowledged that there was the potential for trouble and put a plan into action. When the plane arrived safely at Hartsfield airport, a contingent of police officers was there. We made arrangements for Dr. Lowery and his party to deplane and exit the area to a waiting patrol car on the tarmac. The Klansmen were directed with the rest of the passengers through the normal deplaning procedure. I, of course, continued on my trip to Huntsville but monitored the situation.

This was just one of many examples of how my office of Community Relations worked behind the scenes and out of sight of the public and the press. The most effective work that we have done was done anonymously. There were few reports generated about our work and so there are few records of what really transpired. In a way, we were editing history in real time. We altered the course of events, some of which were certain to have violent endings.

I know about the separation of church and state, but there were many times on the job when I resorted to the one thing I know well. It is the power of prayer. I prayed quite often in tense situations. I prayed for guidance and wisdom to make the right choices. I prayed for the people involved – not just those who look like me – but everyone. I prayed for a safe and peaceful outcome. I could not change what happened in the past. I could however change what will happen in the future. Moment-by-moment, day-by-day, week-by-week, I saw things change. I witnessed history and made history. Some of the stories have been told…many more will never be seen or heard.

FORSYTH COUNTY CONFLICT

For most of my life, Forsyth County was a place where few if any blacks lived. Located about 40 miles north of Atlanta, this rural county with its beautiful rolling hills was harboring a type of hate that dated back decades. The seething undercurrent of racial bigotry there was brought to the forefront after what should have been an enjoyable outing for employees of a public utility. The utility company held an employee picnic at one of the most beautiful lakes in the state – Lake Lanier.

One of the attendees was a black man who was with his wife, who is white. Company officials had no problems with the couple, but people who live in the area did. There was even one reference made by a company employee to the couple that they were not welcome in Forsyth County. After the picnic they were confronted by some of the local residents who reportedly told the man he was not welcome in the county nor was his white wife. There was a small skirmish and the attackers left. We had been informed that the company paid the employee a significant amount of money and the incident was never widely reported.

The history of racism in Forsyth reaches back to the beginning of the 1900's. In 1912 three African American men were accused and convicted of raping a white woman. After the trial, white residents launched a campaign to drive every black person out of the county. Gangs of white men – rode through the county at night terrorizing black families. Crosses were burned. Crops were set ablaze. Shots were fired into homes. Innocent families with small children were threatened, get out of Forsyth County or we will kill you. By the dozens families packed up their belongings and just left. Some forfeited their land. Others sold their property for little or nothing. They were fleeing with little more than their lives and were scarred with the horrible memories that would haunt them the rest of their lives. The campaign of intimidation went on for nearly a month.

The census of 1910 showed there were nearly eleven thousand white residents in Forsyth. There were six hundred and fifty-eight blacks and nearly as many – four hundred and forty – who were classified as mulatto or mixed race. The raids of 1912 pushed all black faces across the borders – out of Forsyth.

By 1930 there were only seventeen black people in the entire county. In the 1960's the threat to people of color lingered. As demonstrations were held across the country involving black people standing up for their rights, in Forsyth they were posting messages aimed at anyone who threatened to change their way of life. Signs were erected in plain view of people arriving in Forsyth. They read "Nigger, don't let the sun set on you in Forsyth County!"

Fast forward fifty-seven years to 1987. The racial climate in Forsyth remained tense for black people, even those who passed through there to do business or for those few people who quietly moved to the area.

The Utility Company incident reignited the issue of race in the county. Charles A. Blackburn, a white resident of Forsyth, owned a small private school there. He had planned to hold a march and rally to draw attention to the issue of race and the fact that there were relatively few blacks living in Forsyth. He wanted to demonstrate that black people can come to the county and would not be harmed. Keep in mind that all around this area – there was increasing growth. The economy was on the upswing in Northern Georgia and families were part of the great suburban sprawl that extended from the heart of Atlanta northward. Blackburn thought he could affect change by holding this rally, but his efforts came to an immediate halt. Just as in 1912, hatred came to bear. Blackburn received threatening phone calls. Word had gotten out that the marches to dispel the image of racism were being planned. No doubt, members of the Ku Klux Klan and other hate groups were determined to keep things the way they were.

Blackburn had recorded the threats on his phone. The nameless, faceless voices said things like:

> "Anti Christ! I got a 30.06 Bullet with your name on it. I just don't think it's a good idea for you to try to get the niggers to come up here. That's why we live in Forsyth County – to get away from them."
> (NYTimes 1/11/87 Dudley Clendinen)

Word had also spread to other counties and to the heart of the civil rights movement, Atlanta, Georgia. The Rev. Hosea Williams and state representative Billy McKinney joined white citizens from counties surrounding Forsyth. They planned to go there and to hold the demonstrations in place of Mr. Blackburn. Other good citizens of Forsyth were also interested in participating.

When the Community Relations Service received confirmation that the march was to take place, I dispatched several people to start doing some background checks on the situation and the people involved. They were to gather newspaper articles, and interviews with people involved including the local sheriff's office. Forsyth County Sheriff Wesley Walraven had confirmed that permits had been issued and he had planned to assign five law enforcement officers to the marchers.

184

The march was set for January 17, 1987. A predetermined route was chosen and everyone was informed of how this was planned to unfold. When members of my team arrived, they were surprised at what they saw. Right there at the planned starting point of the march was a large gathering of people. About 150 white men and women were there. Sprinkled throughout that crowd were some known Klan members, among them David Hammond. Hammond shouted to one of my staff members who knew him all too well, "I am glad the Department of Justice is here to protect my civil and constitutional rights."

The large Greyhound-type bus arrived carrying the protesters of several races. This would surely not end well. Rev. Hosea Williams, Representative Billy McKinney and the other demonstrators got off the bus and were immediately met with slurs and calls for them to go home and not come back. In just a matter of seconds it started. The white protesters hurled a bottle narrowly missing the head of one of the protesters. It smashed against the side of the bus and shattered – raining glass down on the pavement. It was followed by a volley of stones and lumps of rock hard red Georgia clay. With hands and arms covering their heads, the men and women continued to march. The bus driver saw what was happening and fired up his coach and tried to place it between the white mob and the peaceful demonstrators. The bus protected them as they slowly moved along.

The march route included some uneven pavement and places where the sides of the road were hilly. The rock throwers saw this as an opportunity. They could easily place themselves higher than the marchers and could pelt them with whatever they could find or whatever they had brought with them. The six Forsyth county deputies stood there with their nightsticks, their guns and their body protection – not doing anything. They allowed this action to continue. Members of my team from the Community Relations Service and agents from the Georgia Bureau of Investigation tried to intervene. There were only five or six of them. The deputies stayed put. Our team prevailed upon Rev. Williams to put the marchers back on the bus and drive another mile or so down the road away from the mayhem. They chose this option. Five or six Klan members saw what was going on and tried to confront the marchers as they boarded the bus. GBI agents engaged the Klansmen and became involved in a hand to hand combat with them, at times rolling around in the mud. CRS staffer Robert Ensley reported to me that about that time he saw a Klansmen pick up a large rock and tried to hit a black GBI agent in the head. Very quickly Robert rushed to the agent's side and pushed the Klansman down before he could harm the agent. The Klansman's mother was there on the side of the road watching this. She shouted, "That nigger was going to kill my boy!" – referring to the black GBI agent.

Ensley shouted right back, "And I am going to kill him and if you come down here, I will kill you too!"

Agent Moses Ector, an African-American GBI agent was in charge of his group. Had he and his handful of agents not come when they did, most assuredly, some of the marchers would have been killed. The agents were forced to draw their weapons to make the attackers run away.

Everyone made it onto the bus and it sped away. A mile down the road, it stopped and they all got off again. They marched only a short distance and decided they had made their point and opted to leave. Much of the scuffle was caught on videotape. Also clearly visible were the Forsyth county deputies who did nothing to protect the marchers. Only Representative Billy McKinney claimed to be injured, saying his finger had been broken.

Within moments news of what transpired crossed the airways. There were radio reports of the incident and video was flashed across the screens of television sets in Georgia and very quickly around the world. The violence was headline news for several days.

The Southern Christian Leadership Conference leader, Dr. Joseph Lowery made an announcement that this was not the end. Another march would take place the following weekend and this time it would be bigger than before. The demonstrators would not be deterred by the racists' antics of a small group of people.

Knowing of this determination, we assembled a team with specific duties. I contacted the office of Governor Joe Frank Harris. We discussed the possibility of this march being multiple times bigger than the one a week before. We also acknowledged that we had a responsibility to keep the peace, protect everyone involved and allow both sides to exercise their constitutional rights. The governor agreed and we knew that we would need more than local police to protect the crowds and quell any violence.

While I was meeting with the governor, other CRS members were meeting with local law enforcement. It involved city, county and state officers and agents at every level. We developed a contingency plan which would all but guarantee protection of the marchers and of the officers charged with their protection.

The week produced a number of major developments. It was clear that this type of national attention would draw thousands of people. Originally, it was believed that about two thousand people would show up. My experience with protests in the past led me to believe that the number would be closer to ten thousand. I prevailed upon the governor to activate The National Guard and every state trooper, GBI agent and local police officer available.

Media coverage was extensive leading up to the march. There were reports that buses of people from as far away as Washington State and California were on their way. There were also participants from a number of foreign countries including England, Sweden, and Japan. People were in disbelief that in this day and time there was a county where virtually no black people lived. They were even more appalled that violence had struck those people who tried to assemble and demonstrate peacefully.

My goal for this event was to ensure that this was a peaceful event. More than two thousand peace officers and national guardsmen in full tactical gear were there all around the demonstration area. Helicopters provided an aerial view of the activity below. There also was a liberal sprinkling of undercover officers in the crowd prepared to spring into action if needed. This show of force had never been seen in this county.

Early in the morning I arrived at the command center for the event to assess the progress of the security detail. Other members of my team took up positions in other areas of the march zone. The buses began to arrive – some even before dawn. By early afternoon more than twenty thousand civil rights activists had arrived. They were greeted by more than five thousand counter demonstrators. This was the largest gathering of people protesting for civil rights since the sixties.

The day was not without incident. More than 60 people were arrested. Most of them were Klansmen or Klan sympathizers. They continued to harass people in the march and on occasion confronted them physically. GBI agents were swift and moved in quickly, affected an arrest and moved the trouble makers out of the area.

Oprah Winfrey had learned of the attack the previous Saturday watched the developments that week and decided to bring her show to Forsyth for a week of live broadcasts. They involved some of the marchers who were attacked, members of the Klan and also local people who wanted their county portrayed in a positive light.

Among the people on Oprah's show was Frank Shirley, a self proclaimed white supremacist who has been quoted as saying:

> *"Death to the race mixers. They have whirled down the gauntlet at our feet"*
>
> – NYT December 23, 1989

He remained in character on Oprah's broadcast, calling the protesters communists and of low morals.

187

Some townspeople who appeared agreed while others wanted nothing to do with this racist behavior. Members of the CRS team were also there keeping watch over the show and its participants.

The incidents in Forsyth were tailormade for the kinds of services that CRS can provide. We have the ability to get diverse people working together; whether they are private citizens or sometimes competing government agencies, including law enforcement. We also have the expertise to coax those with political power that it is in their best interest to cooperate with federal authorities when necessary to avert problems under their watch. Whoever gave our field representatives the title of conciliator was right on target. Were it not for the cool and analytical heads of this agency, there very well may have been a much more violent scene when the cameras were turned onto Forsyth County, Georgia.

Today that area is one of the fastest growing counties in the state and boasts of a diverse population mixed with those who thought this day would never come.

MY BELOVED
ALPHA PHI ALPHA FRATERNITY, INC.

"You are the might and the strength of the race.
God shall lead you in his grace.
You are the might and strength of the race.
You as an Alpha man set the pace.
Break the shackles.
Break the chains and you shall wear a glorious charm.
Break the shackles break the pains of your father's dreams of liberty.
Strive to build a world that's free.
So onward ye people.
Your people shall bless you.

– Unknown

The poem above aptly describes my relationship with the idea of being a member of Alpha Phi Alpha Fraternity, Inc. For me there was never any consideration of anything else – no other Greek letter organization had ever entered my mind. Alpha is all I know.

My love of Alpha was born on the campus of Philander Smith College. I had returned from serving as a U.S. Marine and as mentioned earlier was pursuing my degree at the Little Rock, Arkansas campus. I had seen the Alpha men and knew of several Alphas who were serving vital roles in the community. I was impressed with these men who were always well dressed, were well educated, and well respected in the community. So I decided this is what I wanted. I needed this type of connection with other positive black men.

I applied and was granted interviews for the possibility of admission. I managed to impress these young men on campus and they allowed me to join the pledge process. There has been a long felt belief that you did not just walk into the fraternity, you were pledged in. Now I was familiar with pledging – after all I am a former Marine. There was no greater pledging than your training in the military. So I was not afraid of this process, although I had made the decision to maintain my dignity and my manhood and not allow anyone to harm me in the process.

189

It was the fall of 1950 and the classes were tough, my work schedule was tough, but the pledging – was, well – Hell! There was an occasion where the brothers brought out the wood. Men in fraternities know what that means. The wooden paddles were used when mistakes were made, history was not known or sometimes for no real reason at all. Whatever, the case, I was not having it.

On one occasion there was a session and the brothers were prepared to punish me. I was called into a room while my line brothers were waiting outside. I entered the room and eyed the brothers there assembled. I raised my voice and said, "Gentlemen, Big Brothers, I have something to say!"

One of the big brothers retorted, "Listen to this dog saying he has something to say!"

Morris Jackson, who was the chapter president, said, "O.K. Let's hear what Ozell has to say to us!"

I was unafraid and in a steady and sustained tone I said, "When I became a pledge and began this process, I was impressed. I was impressed with the commitment to manly deeds, scholarship and love for all mankind! I am a superior student. I love all mankind, but I have not seen that here, and I want you to know that I am not going to take a whipping!"

The dean of pledges walked up right in front of me and locked eyes with mine and said, "What do you mean? What are you trying to say?"

I replied, "I am saying simply this. I mean just what I said. I am not taking a whipping. If anybody hits me, I will fight back. There is nobody in this room who can whip me. I am an ex-marine and I am trained to fight!" Stunned by what I said, the dean of pledges and the president of the chapter thought it best to send me back out of the room.

I went home that night and talked with my mentor and my next door neighbor, attorney Robert Booker. Booker was an Alpha man and he consoled me and then advised me to resign from the pledge process. There were other ways of joining the fraternity. I resigned and was advised to wait till after graduation and then seek membership in the graduate chapter.

I wrote a nice letter to the Pi Lambda Chapter in Little Rock. I explained to them my situation and advised them that I had resigned from the chapter at Philander Smith. I gave them specific reasons for my leaving. I was assured that an invitation would be extended to me based on my explanation. I graduated from Smith in May and in October I became an Alpha man.

I mention this experience because I want other young men to understand that hazing plays no role in any Greek letter organization. It may have been tolerated in the past, but it is prohibited now. Being beaten does not make you a better man.

Let me say that again. Being beaten does not make you a better man. It certainly does not make you a better member of your organization. You become valuable to the fraternity or sorority for that matter through the work you do after you have joined. There is no organization worth dying for.

I am a prime example of this theory. I joined this fraternity for life. I have served on countless committees, and have lead many a mission on behalf of Alpha. Little did I know that this black man who was forced to leave the fraternity would one day hold its highest office – General President.

Alpha has had many a great leader. Many a great man has worn our colors and shield. I have always equated the work of Alpha with the work of the church and the work of any caring man or woman. The fraternity was not designed to exist unto itself, but rather to train leaders who not only run the organization, but also work tirelessly in the community for the greater good of mankind. There is something about the man who embraces these tenets and makes them his own. Brother Peter Clarke said it best when describing an Alpha man:

There Goes An Alpha Man
By: Peter Clarke

There goes a man of high impulse, of princely mien and grace.
There goes a man of humble faith, a credit to his race.
There goes a man of conscious vast, with will to reach his goal.
There goes a man of lordly rank of heroes stock and soul.
There goes a man of noble cast whom hardship cannot break.
There goes a man in merit clad, whom duty won't forsake.
There goes a man of culture verse, who holds a sportsman's creed.
There goes a man too vigilant to bow to lust or greed.
There goes a man whose life is spent in service, not in scorn.
There goes a man whose majesty shines like a may time morn.
There goes a man who is a friend to love and duty truth.
There goes a man to help uplift the lives of wholesome youth.
There goes a man with industry and faith at his command.
There goes the best man in or out for he's an Alpha Man.

While I embrace this sentiment as a proud Alpha man, I must acknowledge that there are also incredible men in other Greek letter organizations who have made significant contributions to this great nation. I thank each of them for what they have done and for also being caring and concerned men.

Perhaps I tried throughout my life to emulate the lives of other great Alpha men, like former Supreme Court Justice Thurgood Marshall, or the great actor Paul Robeson, educator W.E.B. Dubois, Olympic Gold medal winner Jesse Owens, or even the men of my era like former Ambassador to the United Nations Andrew Young and former Atlanta Mayor Maynard Holbrook Jackson. These were men of international import. I was a man who had encountered several of these distinguished individuals and I thought it fitting that the role of our fraternity take on some of the national and international import as its individual members.

I must say one of the men I met who impressed me the most was the late Belford V. Lawson. This man was Alpha personified. Lawson was a very smart man who was born in Roanoke, Virginia. The first thing you noticed about Brother Lawson was the streak of gray that seemed to part his wavy black hair. His eyes were piercing and his erect stature gave him an appearance of being larger than life. That was put into greater perspective when you heard his voice. That amazing ability to speak and to have a room stand still. This had to be the reason he was so successful as a lawyer and a champion for those who were oppressed. Lawson made eight appearances before the U.S. Supreme Court. He taught at Morris Brown College in Atlanta, attended Yale University and finally received his law degree from Howard University in Washington, D.C. In some of his cases, Belford V. Lawson was assisted by Thurgood Marshall. Lawson and Marshall worked together to protect the rights of Negro workers and launched a successful boycott campaign called "Don't Buy Where You Can't Work". He went on to make significant contributions to people of color. He also served as the 16th General President of Alpha Phi Alpha from 1946 – 1951. His oratory skills impressed me beyond words. That is one of the reasons I love to speak. We all want to be a Belford V. Lawson.

I thought of Lawson and many other great leaders in Alpha as I sat in the nominating session of the 74th General Convention in Chicago. General President James R. Williams was presiding. I was currently the Southern regional vice president hailing from the might Eta Lambda Chapter in Atlanta. This would be the most important day to date in my life in Alpha Phi Alpha. I was to be nominated for the position of general president of Alpha.

These sessions are always tense – not knowing whether there would be a "surprise candidate" to emerge in the final moments of nominations. We routinely knew who was running and this would simply codify the nomination according to the rules of the organization. The nominations were nearly complete. Mine had not yet been made when President Williams asked, "Are there any more nominations?"

At that moment, the doors of the convention hall opened and in strode a tall portly light-skinned man with wavy hair. There were gasps in the room because the man who entered was none other than Maynard Holbrook Jackson, the first Black mayor of Atlanta, Georgia. Jackson had reshaped the political landscape of the south and was successful in wresting power from the white establishment in Atlanta to the growing black middle class. His words this moment would shift the power of Alpha.

Jackson raised his hand and was recognized by the floor. "Mr. General President, officers, and brothers here assembled. I rise for the purpose of placing into nomination for 26th General President of Alpha Phi Alpha, a son of the south, a leader in his community, and the baby boy of Lula Belle – Ozell Sutton!"

The room erupted into thunderous applause and chatter. Jackson continued to talk about me and my qualifications for office and almost simultaneously an army of brothers flooded into the room and began passing out pre-printed literature about me and my candidacy. It was a great moment in the history of my life and the beginning of an opportunity for me to be of further service to my fraternity and my country. I was elected handily and was installed as the 26th General President.

There were many triumphs under my administration and I sought to extend the vision of the fraternity, building on the accomplishments of my predecessors. It would have been fruitless for me to mimic other leaders, it was better for me to bring my own skills and assets to the table and carve out a legacy of my own. I would shore up existing programs and introduce new ones.

There were a few accomplishments of which I am most proud. While working with the Department of Justice Office of Community Relations there were a number of major events that affected our people and our children. The most heinous of which had to be the missing and murdered children in Atlanta. For two years there were reports of 29 children who were officially classified into the case known as "The Atlanta Child Murders". I was extremely busy working with local police and community leaders trying to keep the residents calm during this turmoil. It seemed as though no child was safe in the city at that time. That was the fear that gripped this community for such a long time with no suspect and no arrests.

President Ronald Reagan was in the White House at the time and I had made an appeal to the Attorney General's office and the White House to convene a conference on children and to look for ways of establishing a reporting network throughout the country. The murders were happening in Atlanta, but this was a national concern. It could happen in any community in any city, in any state.

One of the greatest lessons Lula Belle ever taught me was when you can't make it one way – find another.

After consulting with the leadership of Alpha Phi Alpha, I decided that if The President won't do it – then Alpha can do it. So Alpha men became involved and helped to coordinate a national summit on children. We raised money from other concerned organizations including the National Conference on Christians and Jews. We held the event in 1981 in Atlanta and after sending out invitations to some of the nation's leaders; we received the support and the presence of three U.S. Senators, five members of the House of Representatives, and well-know child rights advocate, Marian Wright Edleman. We called this the First National Symposium on Missing and Exploited Children. From this became the organization that now looks out for the safety and rights of children around the world. As a footnote, on December 12, 2006, I was named Director Emeritus of the Center. Had it not been for the concern of Alpha men, there may not have been a National Center for Missing & Exploited Children.

I also sought to take Alpha to new heights by keeping the organization on the national scene. Previous General Presidents had done a great job to pushing Alpha beyond the borders of the United States, including programs and relationships with African Nations.

I wanted Alpha to matter to this country. As a result we were instrumental in expanding on the themes of working directly with young people. We partnered with the March of Dimes to establish Project Alpha – a teenage pregnancy prevention program aimed at "the forgotten partner," the teenage boy. In this program we taught personal responsibility and pregnancy prevention using doctors, lawyers, and social and religious professionals.

Knowing that programs were key to growing Alpha, I appointed an energetic young man to serve to the newly created position of Program Specialist. His name was Waldo E. Johnson. His mission was to ensure that Alpha Programs were implemented, funded and executed throughout the country.

Dr. Waldo E. Johnson:
"*General President Ozell Sutton took the stage in Alpha with the determination to advance the organization to newer heights. One of his concerns was always the image of Alpha on the national stage. What you have to know is that in the early 80's black fraternities and sororities were not highly visible organizations. There was this pervasive image of fraternities as being little more than vessels for parties and hazing on college campuses.*

194

Surely people had heard of Alpha but they didn't know Alpha.
Ozell set out to change that image.

In doing so, Ozell made sure to align Alpha Phi Alpha with
already established and recognized entities and made sure there was
publicity surrounding our involvement. At the same time he insured
there were substantive contributions by the Fraternity to organiza-
tions like The Boy Souts of America, The March of Dimes, The
American Cancer Society, The National Urban League, The
National Association for the Advancement of Colored People, and
The United Negro College Fund. In fact Ozell inherited the promise
made by previous administrations to donate a million dollars to
The Urban League, The NAACP and UNCF.

In doing so, Ozell helped to raise the image of the fraternity from
relative obscurity to national prominence. In short order, people
began to listen and they began to call. Countless organizations were
now seeking the help of Alpha Phi Alpha. Worthy as most of the
causes were, we were still a relatively small organization with some
powerful ties and incredible commitment. Service is the threshold of
this organization and Ozell held our feet to the fire and elevated
Alpha to one of the most formidable forces in the country. Today the
effort continues and the reputation of Alpha is at its pinnacle. I am
thankful to Ozell for having planted the seed and for having the
vision to help Alpha live into its greatness with substance and style.

We established a leadership program for high school students in an
effort to train our leaders from the inside. Today this program is known
as the Leadership Development Institute. It was aimed at black boys
who seemed to simply exist in predominately white schools and colleges.
This program would give them life skills that mattered in the social settings
of institutions of higher learning. The first conference was held on the
campus of Morehouse College, and then to Fisk University and then to other
college campuses across the country.

These accomplishments as leader of Alpha are not so much a reflection on me,
but rather a testament to brotherhood. I have made some great friendships in
Alpha. Sure we share the common bond of the organization, but it goes further
than that. It extends to my beliefs as an African-American man, to my desires for
the betterment of man and his condition, and certainly to my love of country and
its people.

It is difficult to put into words what Alpha Phi Alpha means to me. This organization has been such an integral part of my professional, personal, and spiritual life. I recall one of my personal greatest moments. It was in the summer of 2006. Thousands upon thousands of college-educated black men gathered in Washington, D.C. to commemorate the 100th anniversary of the founding of Alpha. Each day brought new and lasting memories for me – seeing familiar faces of Alpha men who have been there, some for decades; meeting brothers I have never met before and the unmeasured love that we all have for each other and the organization that so binds our hearts to beat in the same rhythm. I remember now with a tear in my eye, the moment my name was called in a fraternal meeting and I was asked to offer some reflections on Alpha as the 26th General President. Here is a portion of my reflections before the assembly:

> You have allowed me to walk among and to be one of you and you have supported me and for that I am eternally grateful.
>
> If I were a clergy, Brother Shannon, I would take a verse from the eighth number from the Book of Psalms, and in the words of the great Psalmist David I would say, 'What is man that though art mindful of him?'
>
> And if I were a politician – I would build my platform on one of the greatest documents ever conceived in the human heart and I would say as in the forefathers – that 'We hold these truths to be self evident that all men are created equal...'
>
> And these two documents one from the bible and one from the early life of this country have been two guiding principles in my life.
>
> ...I was beaten in Little Rock when I helped to escort 'The Nine' into Little Rock High School. I was beaten in Birmingham when we marched in Birmingham. I was beaten when we crossed the Edmund Pettus Bridge. And I was beaten in the last protest that Martin led in Memphis....you remember the protest with the garbage workers before he died...
>
> And I look back at it...every man who hit me during those demon-strations is dead....and I am still here...still standing...
>
> And part of that is because of you... I had a home outside of the struggle that gave me strength....and sometimes assistance...and that home was Alpha Phi Alpha Fraternity...
>
> No matter my circumstance – good or bad Alpha was there to support me – even before I became your General President. I thank

you for the opportunity to serve, but most of all I thank you for the brotherhood we all share.

Thank you to the brothers of Alpha Phi Alpha without whom Ozell Sutton would simply be Lula Belle's baby boy.

EPILOGUE

The words on the preceding pages chronicle just a fraction of my life and the life and times of our country. I often wondered how I would end this story. What would I say at the end that could serve not as a summary, but more of a challenge? I have not sought to embarrass or ridicule any one particular race gender or creed. I have, however, tried to shed some light on the inner workings of some of the major events that fill the pages of our history. I guess, in a way, these are the untold stories.

To bring this whole thing full circle, I would have to say that I am haunted by the challenges that were set before me. Haunted is the right word because the cries of my people would sometimes keep me up at night. I would become restless in those wee hours of the stillest of evenings. Their cries tore at my comfort and called me to get up and get going and to do something. They charged me with the responsibility to be of service. The writer who helped me with this story, my fraternity brother and my friend, heard me say many a time as we sat in the basement of my home, "Victor, you know this is my life's calling because I have a charge to keep."

Ironically those are the words to a song that is the testament upon which I have built this life and they were written by another Alpha Man, Charles Wesley.

A CHARGE TO KEEP I HAVE

A charge to keep I have,
A God to glorify,
A never-dying soul to save,
And fit it for the sky.

To serve the present age,
My calling to fulfill:
O may it all my powers engage
To do my Master's will!

Arm me with jealous care,
As in Thy sight to live;

199

And O Thy servant, Lord, prepare
A strict account to give!
Help me to watch and pray,
And on Thyself rely,
Assured, if I my trust betray,
I shall for ever die.

Thus, on this I stand and now I offer the challenge to you. I look around this world and I am disturbed by what I see.

I see people in Sierra Leone whose hands have been chopped off to keep them from voting. But stop them it does not – they find a way to cast their ballots in the democratic process. Here at home we celebrate a "high" voter turnout when we surpass 40 percent of the registered voters casting their ballots. What a sin! We must do better. People died for this right. Persons in other countries are dying today for the same thing we take for granted.

I have seen students fail a test and then simply give up. They would score poorly on the SAT and then throw in the towel. Did Martin stop because he was arrested, his life threatened, a cross burned in his front yard just feet from where his children were sleeping? Did John Lewis stop after he was beaten by white mobs in Montgomery? Did those children stop attending class because each and every day they were taunted in the halls of Central High School? We have somehow lost our way. We are lost...but we can be redeemed. We have a generation of bright and brilliant young minds right there before us, just like those kids at Frederick Douglass High School. Their potential is immeasurable, but we have to reassure them and nurture them and admonish them and lead them.

I can never profess to tell you how you should worship. I believe in God. I know what He has done for me. I know what He can do for you. I say that because we have an entire generation of children who know not what it means to go to Sunday school or to church service. They have no belief in a higher power and I surmise they also have no hope. We must let them know that things do not happen all on their own.

I say to cleave to the God who brought us over a mighty long way and never remove your hand from his side.

Father, I stretch my hands to Thee,
No other help I know;

If Thou withdraw Thyself from me,
Ah! whither shall I go?

What did Thine only Son endure,
Before I drew my breath!
What pain, what labor, to secure
My soul from endless death!

Surely Thou canst not let me die;
O speak, and I shall live;
And here I will unwearied lie,
Till Thou Thy Spirit give.

Author of faith! to Thee I lift
My weary, longing eyes:
O let me now receive that gift!
My soul without it dies.

And so this little servant, Ozell Sutton, leaves you right here.. Be good and kind to people and always be the protector of the civil rights we so ardently worked to protect. Never forget those who made it their mission to be the trailblazers for freedom.

I have been to many a great hall adorned with statues of great people. I have toured many a museum bearing the names of philanthropists and architects and designers. I have seen monuments spiraling toward the sky. Each one of these has this in common. Not one is dedicated to a man or woman who didn't try. There are no markers or highways dedicated to those who were afraid. There is no page in history dedicated to those who chose to retreat and cower in their homes. Make your mark – large or small – and make it count for someone.

I am Ozell Sutton and it is a mighty long way – *From Yonder to Here.*

A Note From The Author
Vic Carter

As much as this book is about Ozell Sutton, it is more about everyone who reads it. It is the untold story of an America that yearns to rid itself of a horrible past. I forgot what movie I was watching, but there was this one line where one man asks another, "Will God ever forgive us for what we have done to each other?" Wow! Right there in the darkened viewing room in my basement I began to think about all the horrible things that people endure each and every day, many times at the hands of another person. How could God's greatest creations be so mean to each other? And then I think about people like Ozell. In the course of writing this book I encountered a number of people from his era who had made contributions to this country during some of its darkest days. They had literally suffered at the hands of other human beings, atrocities too horrible for words. Those were people who had sacrificed of themselves for civil rights, for better schools, for cleaner neighborhoods, for the right to vote. Throughout my career, as a newsman, I have met many of these people. Thurgood Marshall, Benjamin Hooks, Congressman John Lewis, former U.N. Ambassador Andrew Young, Coretta Scott King, Roy Wilkins, Jesse Jackson, and on and on and on. There is no possible way that their entire stories will ever be told. Then there are those people we do not know, who never made it into a headline, but nevertheless served vital roles in the history of this nation. Some of them chose to remain nameless and faceless. Others were simply ignored and were never given their due. These are the people who helped to make America great, who did the "grass roots" work that is so critical to any movement, any project, any endeavor. To them I say "Thank You". Thank you for coming this way and doing what you did.

I also have to make a note about the role of Alpha Phi Alpha Fraternity, Inc. in my life. I am of the firm belief that if a small group of African American men on the campus of Morehead State University had not approached me about joining their efforts to charter a chapter there, I would not be the man I am today. There on that tiny Appalachian campus a seed was planted. It grew into a chapter of A-Phi-A and its members joined the legions of other men who shared the same ideas and values and commitment to people.

I have to pay special thanks to those Alpha Men in Lynchburg, Va. and Raleigh, North Carolina, and Atlanta, Georgia, and Columbia, MD who hold me up in the name of Alpha. You see the brotherhood of Alpha Phi Alpha has a way of changing your life. It puts you in the company of men who have already been there and those who are on their way. I grew the most as a man while in the great Eta Lambda Chapter in Atlanta, Georgia. In that room there were men who sat next to you and told you how things were done. They included two mayors of the city, Andrew Young and Maynard Jackson. They included the presidents of colleges and universities. There were magnates of business, physicians, bankers, lawyers, educators, scientists, and every other walk of life. Each of these men left their titles and credentials at the door and entered a room where they were simply servants of the organization. These men ran efficient meetings and tackled massive problems with sound and workable solutions. They were civic minded and knew we did not exist unto ourselves, but were mandated to be of service to others in our community, our state, our country and in our world.

I thank these men for seeing something in me, for putting me to work for the organization, and for showing me the way. They built my confidence, just by being there. These men were there for each other in a way unlike anything I have ever seen. That is where I learned, understood, and embraced brotherhood. I dare say this same sentiment exists in other Greek letter organizations. However, my partiality dictates that I acknowledge Alpha Phi Alpha as the pattern by which others measure themselves.

I was made by Alpha; not the organization, but by the men who wear its name. I am a product of Alpha, not the founders who organized in 1906, but by the men who carry forth its mandates. I am the legacy of Alpha, not the letters intertwined, but the brothers who grow men and leaders and doers.

Yes – this is Ozell's book, but he is the image of the man we all want to be. So his story becomes our story. Thank you Ozell for writing these chapters in history and paving a way for a little black boy from Radford, Virginia to be able to sit in the anchor chair at the top of Television Hill and now to write the story of a man who helped to shape this land we call America.. You inspire us all – that no matter what, we can make it...*From Yonder to Here!*

ACKNOWLEDGEMENTS

Dr. Ozell Sutton, Vic Carter and Lee-Com Media, LLC wish to acknowledge the contributions of the following persons to this project:

Cover Design by:
Jossan Robinson – Design 1320, LLC

Cover Photos:
Brincent Lee & Archives of the Library of Congress

Other photographs donated by:
Ozell Sutton

White House Photos by:
Marteze Hammond & Vic Carter

Copy Editing by:
Mrs. Evelyn Floyd, Charlotte, N.C.

Printed by:
Litho Impressions, Inc., Temple Hills, MD

Special Thanks to:
Mr. Georg Iggers
Mr. Earl Daniels
Former Atlanta Mayor and Ambassador Andrew Young
The Reverend Jesse Jackson
Mr. Benjamin Hooks
Mr. Darryl R. Matthews
Mr. Herman Skip Mason, Jr.